MIKE MENTZER'S
NUTRITIONAL PHILOSOPHY

You Can't Out-Train a Bad Diet

Contents

4

Introduction

Mike Mentzer, a name that rings with an air of enigma, irreverence, and a dash of audacity. The man was no less than a revolutionary figure in the bodybuilding world, exploding onto the scene with his Mr. Universe win and a perfect score to boot. Known best for his adamant advocacy of High-Intensity Training, or HIT, he disrupted the norm, challenging the gospel of endless hours in the gym with a radical regimen that promised results with a fraction of the time investment. And while Mentzer's training philosophies have often eclipsed the conversation, what's equally compelling but less discussed is the role of nutrition in his approach to bodybuilding.

When most people engage in the discussion of Mike Mentzer's bodybuilding philosophy, they dive headfirst into the technicalities of HIT—how to lift, when to lift, and how much rest is required between lifts. Yet, if you dig deeper into his teachings and interviews, you'll find that Mentzer wasn't just a master of muscle fatigue; he was an aficionado of feeding those muscles correctly. It's as if each chiseled muscle was a canvas and nutrition was the invisible hand, painting in the intricate details. He believed that nutrition wasn't just an accompaniment to a workout regimen; it was a fundamental pillar. You can't build Rome in a day, and you certainly can't build it with brittle bricks and shoddy mortar. In the same vein, Mentzer felt that you can't create a sculpted physique without paying meticulous attention to what fuels it.

When it came to the fundamentals—protein, carbohydrates, fats—Mentzer offered a perspective that was surprisingly traditional yet radically individualistic. For him, proteins were the building blocks, but not just any protein would do. He wanted protein that would serve the body best: quality over quantity. There was no room for compromises, and Mentzer's approach hinged on the optimal—optimal sources, optimal timing, and optimal preparation. Carbohydrates, often demonized by fad diets, found refuge in his nutrition philosophy. He acknowledged the essential role they played in high-intensity training, as energy providers, as fuel that allowed you to push that extra set, lift that extra pound.

Let's not forget fats. For Mentzer, the narrative around fats needed a serious overhaul. In an era that often demonized fat, labeling it the harbinger of all ailments, he recognized its crucial role in hormonal balance. He talked about fats as if they were the misunderstood rebels of the nutrient world—necessary, beneficial, but often misused. He didn't advise avoiding fats; he advised understanding them. Differentiating between good fats that provide essential fatty acids and the bad ones that led to arterial plaque was critical. One size doesn't fit all, and Mentzer was keen to impress upon his followers that the macro ratio that worked wonders for one might be entirely counterproductive for another. Individualization was his mantra, not just in training but in nutritional habits as well. After all, what's the point of a rigorous, personalized training program if it's coupled with a one-size-fits-all diet?

But what about the nuts and bolts, the actual implementation of these lofty ideals? Mike Mentzer wasn't a man to leave you hanging. While he may not have spelled out an A-Z diet plan for the masses, his teachings did touch on practical aspects. Meal timing, for instance, was a topic that he didn't skirt around. And why would he? It's integral to fueling a body geared for high-intensity performance. Pre- and post-workout nutrition became not just a supplement to the training but a part of the training itself. Yet, even here, Mentzer pulled no punches. He scoffed at rigidly structured six-meal-a-day plans, the gospel according to conventional bodybuilding wisdom. For him, when you ate should align with what your body tells you, not what the clock dictates.

And then there was the question of supplements—the Pandora's box of bodybuilding nutrition. To pop or not to pop? In a realm rife with magic pills and miracle powders, Mentzer offered a clear-eyed perspective. Supplements could play a role, yes, but they were just that: supplemental. They weren't substitutes for a well-rounded, meticulously planned diet. A whey protein shake could aid in recovery, but it couldn't replace a balanced meal. A pre-workout could fire you up, but it couldn't make up for a poorly planned diet.

As for those looking for a detailed menu, a step-by-step diet guide from the high priest of HIT himself, well, they'd likely be disappointed. Mentzer may have had strong views on the quality of food and its vital role in bodybuilding, but he wasn't going to spoon-feed anyone. The core of his philosophy was self-experimentation, a concept that extended from his HIT principles right into his nutrition ethos. Just as no two bodies respond the same way to a set of bicep curls, no two bodies metabolize nutrients identically. For Mentzer, the journey to nutritional nirvana was paved with self-discovery. Each individual had to play the scientist, the subject, and the analyst, tailoring their diet according to personal needs, observing changes, and optimizing accordingly.

A Brief Biography of Mike Mentzer

Mike Mentzer, born on November 15, 1951, in Pennsylvania, was a renowned American IFBB professional bodybuilder, author, and businessman. His journey in bodybuilding began at the young age of 11, inspired by muscle magazine covers. Mentzer's father supported his interest by providing a set of weights and an instruction booklet. Adhering to the booklet's advice, he trained no more than three days a week. By 15, Mentzer's body weight had reached 165 lbs, and he could bench press 370 lbs. His early goal was to emulate his bodybuilding hero, Bill Pearl.

Mentzer's competitive bodybuilding career started at 18, with his first contest in 1969. He experienced significant success, including winning the 1976 Mr. America title and the heavyweight division of the 1978 IFBB Mr. Universe. His encounter with Casey Viator, the winner of a bodybuilding contest, led him to meet and be influenced by Arthur Jones, the pioneer of high-intensity training principles. These principles emphasized strict form, slow and controlled weight movements, working muscles to complete failure, and avoiding overtraining. Mentzer, intrigued by these concepts, began implementing and refining them in his own training.

In 1979, Mentzer achieved a major milestone by winning the heavyweight class of the Mr. Olympia with a perfect 300 score, although he lost the overall title to Frank Zane. The following year, he placed fourth in a tie at the 1980 Mr. Olympia, after which he retired from competitive bodybuilding at 29. Despite his retirement, Mentzer remained a prominent figure in the bodybuilding world, questioning certain contest results and maintaining an amicable relationship with fellow bodybuilder Arnold Schwarzenegger.

Mentzer's bodybuilding philosophy was heavily influenced by Arthur Jones' high-intensity training concepts, which he sought to perfect. He believed in brief, infrequent, and intense weight training to achieve the best results in the shortest time. This approach was detailed in his final work, "High-Intensity Training the Mike Mentzer Way." Mentzer also emphasized the importance of critical thinking and reasoning in both bodybuilding and life. He advocated for a balanced life, where bodybuilding was one of many worthwhile pursuits.

Nutrition was a key component of Mentzer's philosophy. In his book "Heavy Duty Nutrition," he argued that nutrition for athletes need not be as extreme as often portrayed in the bodybuilding industry. He recommended well-balanced diets and emphasized the role of carbohydrates as a major part of caloric intake. His approach was based on the simple logic that muscle growth required a modest surplus of calories, mainly from non-protein sources.

Mentzer's Heavy Duty program initially involved 7–9 sets per workout, three times a week. However, with the evolution of bodybuilding in the early 1990s, he modified this approach to include fewer sets and more rest days. This modification, termed the 'Ideal (Principled) Routine,' emphasized minimal training with maximum recovery time. Techniques like forced reps, negative reps, and rest-pause were employed to push sets beyond failure. Mentzer underscored the importance of intensity over duration in training for muscle hypertrophy.

Throughout his career, Mentzer made significant contributions to the bodybuilding community, inspiring many with his unique approach to training and nutrition. His legacy continues to influence bodybuilders and fitness enthusiasts worldwide. His induction into the IFBB Hall of Fame in 2002 was a testament to his impact on the sport.

Overview of High Intensity Training (HIT)

High Intensity Training's origins are firmly rooted in the quest for maximizing results in minimal time. Its conception stems from a rebellion against traditional lengthy workout sessions. Over time, as athletes and trainers began to observe the undeniable results of HIT, it became clear that the methodology had merits that went beyond saving time. The evolution of HIT has seen its share of critics and skeptics. Still, like any revolutionary approach, it has carved out its niche in the fitness realm, not merely as a fad but as a compelling alternative.

Delving into the science behind HIT gives us insight into its efficacy. At its core, HIT zeroes in on the body's fast-twitch muscle fibers. These fibers, unlike their slow twitch counterparts, have a higher capacity for growth and strength. By engaging these fibers to their maximum potential in shorter periods, HIT ensures optimal muscle engagement. The result? Enhanced muscle growth and strength in a fraction of the time. Now, this isn't magic or some gimmicky shortcut. It's rooted in hard biological facts about how our muscles function and respond to stimuli.

Why then HIT? Isn't traditional training effective? The answer lies not in dismissing traditional methods but in highlighting HIT's unique advantages. At the forefront is improved muscle efficiency. With HIT, muscles learn to operate at their peak in shorter bursts, leading to enhanced performance even outside the gym. Furthermore, the concise nature of HIT sessions means one spends less time working out, freeing up time for other pursuits. Additionally, the metabolic response to such workouts is phenomenal. The body continues to burn calories at an elevated rate long after the workout is done, a phenomenon often referred to as the 'afterburn' effect.

The efficacy of HIT is not merely in the physical realm. It demands a mental synergy, an unparalleled mind muscle connection. Each rep in a HIT workout requires focus, intent, and visualization. It's not about mindlessly lifting a weight but visualizing the muscle at work, feeling every fiber engage, and channeling one's energy into that singular effort. Mike Mentzer often emphasizes that the success of a HIT routine is 50% physical and 50% mental.

With such a demanding regimen, setting clear, tangible goals becomes indispensable. Without a defined 'why,' the intensity can quickly become directionless. Be it packing on muscle, bolstering strength, or enhancing stamina, every HIT enthusiast needs a beacon, a guiding light. Knowing why you're pushing your limits, why you're subjecting your body to such intense stress, gives purpose to the pain.

As with any journey, knowing where you stand and how far you've come is crucial. Mike Mentzer has always been an advocate of meticulous progress tracking. Whether it's jotting down the weights lifted, snapping progress photos, or simply gauging how one feels post workout, documenting the journey is pivotal. It offers both motivation and a roadmap for adjustments.

Preparation is paramount in HIT. It's not about diving headfirst into intensity but understanding and mastering the nuances of form and technique. The emphasis is always on how you lift rather than the sheer weight. An improper form can be counterproductive and potentially dangerous. A 20-pound weight lifted with impeccable form can yield better results and is safer than a 50-pound weight heaved carelessly.

Warming up might seem elementary, yet its significance in HIT is monumental. With such explosive, intense sessions, priming the body is not optional; it's mandatory. A HIT-specific warm-up ensures that the muscles, joints, and cardiovascular system are all in sync and ready for the onslaught.

Safety cannot be overemphasized. The sheer intensity of HIT means the margin for error is minimal. The risk of injuries escalates if one doesn't adhere to safety protocols. Recognizing one's limits, choosing the right weights, ensuring proper form, and most importantly, knowing when to stop are non negotiable aspects of HIT.

Now, with any innovative approach comes a slew of myths. One pervasive myth surrounding HIT is equating longer gym hours with better outcomes. This fallacy often stems from the age-old belief that hard work is directly proportional to time spent. However, HIT stands as a testament to the fact that efficiency and intensity can truncate workout durations without compromising results.

Another rampant misunderstanding is the very essence of intensity in HIT. Many assume it's about pushing oneself to the brink every single time, flinging weights around with wild abandon. This couldn't be further from the truth. True intensity is measured, controlled, and purposeful. It's about challenging the muscles, not annihilating them.

A common critique thrown at HIT is the specter of overtraining. Critics argue that such relentless intensity inevitably leads to burnout. But what they often overlook is the emphasis HIT places on recovery. It's not about hammering the muscles daily. It's about short, intense bursts followed by adequate recovery, allowing muscles to repair and grow.

Embarking on the HIT journey is no casual undertaking. It demands a level of commitment that transcends mere physical exertion. It's a symphony of mind and body, where both have to be in perfect harmony. As one prepares to delve deeper into HIT's intricacies, the words of Mike Mentzer serve as a guiding principle: "Intensity is not just about the weight on the bar; it's about the weight of your intent and focus."

Importance of Balance in Nutrition

B uilding a formidable physique isn't just about lifting weights; it's about fueling your body with a balanced blend of essential nutrients. This is where the balanced macronutrient approach, or the 60-25-15 diet, becomes pivotal. This strategic eating plan emphasizes a proportional intake of carbohydrates, proteins, and fats – the critical trio for optimal health and vitality. By advocating for 60% of your daily calories from carbohydrates, 25% from protein, and 15% from fats, this diet aligns with the wisdom of Mike Mentzer and numerous nutrition experts.

Mentzer, a proponent of this approach, stressed the importance of planning your diet to match these ratios, echoing the guidelines of esteemed nutritionists and the Senate Subcommittee on Nutrition. This diet isn't just popular for its simplicity; it's effective in managing body weight and enhancing overall health. The key lies in its balanced distribution of macronutrients, fostering weight management, boosting energy levels, and promoting general well-being.

For those looking to adopt this diet, the journey begins with determining your daily caloric needs. Once established, you can allocate your calories in the 60-25-15 pattern. In a 2,000-calorie diet, this translates to 1,200 calories from carbohydrates, 500 from proteins, and 300 from fats. This disciplined approach to nutrition underscores that bodybuilding is as much about what you eat as it is about your training regimen.

The 60-25-15 diet isn't a mere guideline; it's a foundation for building a strong, healthy body. By understanding and implementing this balanced nutrient approach, you're not just lifting weights in the gym, you're building a robust, resilient body capable of withstanding the demands of intensive training. This diet makes you rethink nutrition, not as a secondary aspect of bodybuilding, but as a primary, integral component. With this approach, every meal becomes a step towards achieving a physique that's not just about muscle, but also about health and vitality.

The Trials of Youth

Mike Mentzer's bodybuilding career, when viewed retrospectively, is marked by a significant journey from confusion to enlightenment. As a young, enthusiastic bodybuilder, starting at the age of 12, Mentzer spent many years enveloped in what he called, "ignorance and delusions." His primary source of information were muscle magazines, which he read voraciously, and their alluring advertisements. These sources misleadingly suggested that achieving the status of Mr. America was an easy feat, attainable almost overnight with the right investments in certain products.

One notable example of this deception was an advertisement promising muscle gains of a pound a day by consuming a specific drink. Mentzer, young and impressionable, was completely taken in by this claim. His dedication to this approach led him to increase his weight from 180 to 250 pounds within seven months, with most of the weight gain being body fat. This rapid increase in size brought its own set of challenges. The financial strain of his diet led to his mother being unable to afford his milk consumption, which had escalated to nearly two gallons a day. Moreover, Mentzer started noticing disturbing stretch marks on his body and faced the inconvenience of outgrowing his clothes rapidly. This situation reached a turning point when his father refused to buy him more clothes, effectively ending his phase of excessive bulking.

The following six months were spent in an attempt to reverse the damage. The prevailing bodybuilding strategy at the time was to bulk up and then trim down, with the goal of maximizing weight gain regardless of its composition, and then shedding the fat to reveal underlying muscle. However, this approach proved counterproductive for Mentzer. After an extended period of cutting and trimming, he found himself weighing less than his initial 180 pounds. The excessive weight loss, attributed to starvation and overtraining, led to a reduction in muscle mass, leaving him with less muscle than when he started his bulking journey.

Throughout the years, Mentzer remained committed to his dream of becoming an accomplished bodybuilder. He closely followed every new fad diet and bodybuilding trend. However, he encountered a significant contradiction in the bodybuilding community.

The same sources that had been selling products and methods were now suggesting that bodybuilding lacked exactness, with no universal principles or truths. This revelation led Mentzer to question whether bodybuilding could truly be considered a science, as it seemed to require individualized approaches for training and nutrition. This realization marked a pivotal point in Mentzer's understanding and approach to bodybuilding, leading him towards a more informed and critical perspective on the sport.

A Unique Philosophy

Mike Mentzer stood out for in the bodybuilding world for his unique approach to training and nutrition, which he believed was rooted in scientific principles. Mentzer claimed to be the only top bodybuilder who approached both training and nutrition from a scientific standpoint. This bold assertion stemmed from his observation that most top bodybuilders acknowledged the individual differences in training and nutritional requirements, a concept he found unscientific. In contrast, Mentzer held the view that everyone is fundamentally similar, with nearly identical training and nutritional needs, positioning himself as a potentially scientific bodybuilder.

Contrary to the belief that bodybuilding is devoid of scientific basis, Mentzer argued that the discipline is indeed a science, grounded in the established principles of exercise physiology and nutritional science. He emphasized that nutrition is not a universal concept applied uniformly to all, but rather a personalized science. This science takes into account individual factors such as genetics, lifestyle, and specific health goals. Through his journey, Mentzer aimed to demystify nutrition by distinguishing between nutritional myths and evidence-based truths. This demystification process was crucial in empowering individuals to make informed dietary choices.

Mike Mentzer's unique perspective on bodybuilding as a scientific discipline challenged the prevailing notions in the field. He advocated for a more enlightened approach to training and nutrition, merging scientific knowledge with practical insights. This approach recognizes the complex and dynamic interaction between food and the human body, moving beyond the limited scope of just calorie counting or blindly following the latest dietary trends. It acknowledges the highly individual nature of nutritional needs, influenced by a variety of factors including age, gender, genetics, lifestyle, and overall health.

A fundamental aspect of bodybuilding nutrition is the understanding that food is not solely a fuel source. Instead, it's a rich source of macro and micronutrients, each playing a critical role in various physiological functions. This perspective emphasizes the importance of consuming a diverse range of whole, nutrient-dense foods, while also considering the practicalities and cultural aspects that influence eating habits.

Nutritional in bodybuilding must acknowledge the value of balance and moderation. One must advocate against extreme or restrictive diets that may be unsustainable in the long term and detrimental to overall well-being. This viewpoint challenges the classification of foods into 'good' or 'bad' categories, promoting a more holistic view of diet that avoids rigid rules and guilt associated with occasional indulgences.

Another key element is the awareness of how food processing affects nutritional quality, along with the importance of understanding food labels. This knowledge is vital in an era rife with misinformation and fad diets, helping bodybuilders and fitness enthusiasts discern evidence-based information from sensational claims.

Embracing nutrition in bodybuilding means recognizing that nutritional needs are not static but evolve over time and under different circumstances. It encourages a sustainable, realistic approach to health, urging individuals to develop a positive, adaptable relationship with food that respects their unique biological and lifestyle needs. By adopting this approach, bodybuilders can navigate the complexities of dietary choices, leading to a more informed, personalized, and effective nutrition strategy for their training and overall well-being.

The Role of Nutrition in Achieving Optimal Physique

Achieving optimal nutrition for building lean muscle mass requires a well-rounded and meticulous approach. This strategy includes a focus on proper distribution of macronutrients, adequate intake of micronutrients, and the strategic timing of meals to support muscle growth and overall health.

Protein stands at the forefront of a muscle-building nutrition plan. As a critical component for muscle repair and growth, it's essential to consume adequate protein from a variety of sources. These sources can include lean meats, poultry, fish, eggs, and dairy, along with plant-based options such as legumes and tofu. This diverse intake ensures the body receives all necessary amino acids for muscle protein synthesis. By Mike's calculation, muscle composition includes about 70% water, 22% protein, 6% lipids, and 2% inorganic materials, highlighting the importance of protein in muscle structure.

Carbohydrates are equally crucial in a bodybuilder's diet. They play a significant role in replenishing glycogen stores, which are vital for fueling intense workouts and supporting muscle function. Opting for complex carbohydrates, found in whole grains, fruits, and vegetables, provides a steady energy release, beneficial for sustained performance.

Healthy fats, sourced from foods like avocados, nuts, seeds, and olive oil, are important for hormone production and overall health maintenance. Contrasting muscle composition with that of fat, which contains approximately 15% water, 12% protein, 70% lipids, and 3% inorganic materials, underscores the different roles and requirements of these tissue types in the body.

Micronutrients, including vitamins and minerals such as vitamin D, calcium, magnesium, and iron, play pivotal roles in bone health, energy metabolism, and oxygen transport. These elements are integral to the muscle-building process and overall body function.

Hydration, often overlooked, is essential for peak performance and recovery. Ensuring adequate water intake supports various bodily functions and can enhance training outcomes.

Meal timing, particularly focusing on pre- and post-workout nutrition, is key for optimizing nutrient absorption and muscle recovery. Consuming the right balance of nutrients before and after training can significantly impact muscle development and recovery processes.

Tailoring nutrition to individual needs is paramount in bodybuilding. Factors like body composition, training intensity, and personal goals must be considered to develop a successful and sustainable approach to lean muscle building. Consulting with a registered dietitian or nutritionist can provide personalized guidance and ensure that the nutrition plan supports both specific bodybuilding objectives and long-term health.

crafting a balanced muscle-building diet is a complex task that demands meticulous consideration of macronutrient ratios, micronutrient needs, and caloric balance, tailored to the individual's specific goals and physiological requirements.

Protein, the bedrock of muscle growth, must be consumed in adequate amounts to facilitate muscle protein synthesis. Bodybuilders are advised to incorporate a variety of protein sources, including lean meats, poultry, fish, dairy, and plant-based options such as legumes and tofu. This diverse intake ensures a comprehensive amino acid profile, crucial for effective muscle repair and growth.

Carbohydrates are indispensable in a muscle-building diet, serving as the primary energy source for intense workouts and aiding in glycogen replenishment. Opting for complex carbohydrates, found in whole grains, fruits, and vegetables, ensures a steady release of energy and helps prevent energy dips during and after workouts.

Healthy fats, sourced from foods like avocados, nuts, seeds, and olive oil, play a vital role in hormone production and joint health. They should be incorporated in moderation to maintain a balanced macronutrient profile.

The intricate balance of these macronutrients must be attuned to each individual's unique needs and bodybuilding goals. Alongside macronutrients, micronutrients hold significant importance; deficiencies in vitamins and minerals can hinder muscle development and overall performance. Vitamins such as D, and minerals like calcium and magnesium, are essential for bone health, while iron is crucial for effective oxygen transport in the body.

Hydration is another critical yet often overlooked aspect of a muscle-building diet. Adequate water intake is vital for optimal muscle function and recovery, especially in the physically demanding routine of bodybuilding.

Caloric intake needs to be carefully managed depending on the specific objectives of the bodybuilder. This may involve a caloric surplus for muscle mass gain or a slight deficit to lose fat while preserving muscle tissue.

Meal timing, particularly around workout sessions, plays a significant role. Properly planned pre- and post-workout meals can greatly influence energy levels during training and subsequent recovery.

For bodybuilders, regular assessments and adjustments to their diet are essential. This dynamic approach, often enhanced with professional guidance from dietitians or nutritionists, helps in fine-tuning the nutrition plan. This not only aids in sustained muscle building but also ensures overall health and well-being. By adopting these strategies, bodybuilders can create a balanced dietary regimen that supports their training objectives and promotes long-term physical health.

The Importance Pre-Workout and Post-Workout Nutrition

High-Intensity Training (HIT) without a calculated, approach to nutrition is like a Lamborghini with no gas. All potential, no performance. People think they can pump iron until their muscles cry for mercy and that's it—job done, physique made. Nothing could be more off-target. Nutrition isn't just the cornerstone of your HIT strategy; it's the foundation upon which everything else is built.

Alright, I hear you: "But what's so critical about pre-workout nutrition? I've got my routine down." Well, your "routine" is underachieving if you haven't dialed in your pre-workout nutrition. Think of your body like a high-performance sports car. Would you head into a Grand Prix with just any fuel? Hell no, you wouldn't. A high-octane race calls for high-octane fuel. A pre-workout meal isn't just food; it's your primary ammunition. You're looking at carbohydrates for quick energy and proteins for sustained release. Simple carbs can give you that quick burst, while complex carbs sustain you through that grueling HIT session. And protein? Don't even get me started. It's not just for post-workout; having it beforehand ensures you're not cannibalizing your muscles. Oh, and fats—remember, they're not your enemy here. A small amount can actually support hormone balance. That's your testosterone, your adrenaline—the stuff that turns you from an average Joe into a HIT beast.

By this point, if you're not prioritizing your pre-workout meal, you're setting yourself up for a hard road. I don't care how hardcore your workout is; you'll hit that wall sooner or later. But guess what? Once you're pounding out those final reps, dripping sweat, and adrenaline is buzzing through your veins, your job isn't done. Anyone who thinks the HIT session's end means it's time to relax is misguided. That's like saying, "Well, I got to the finish line; it doesn't matter if I collapse now." It does matter. What comes next is so critically important that it can make or break all the effort you've just put in.

For the post-workout phase, it's all about two things: recovery and growth. Your muscles are like a battleground after a war. It's chaos in there—fibers torn, glycogen depleted, screaming for nutrients. Give them what they need or your HIT efforts are like throwing water into a sieve—pointless. A protein source is essential. We're talking a fast-absorbing protein, like whey, to kick-start muscle recovery. You've got this tiny window—about an hour or so post-workout—where your body is a nutrient-absorbing sponge. You must capitalize on it. Slam down that protein shake, eat that chicken breast, do what you have to, but get that protein in. Don't forget carbs. Your muscles are depleted; they've burnt through glycogen like a wildfire through dry grass. You need to replenish. A quick carb source—yes, even sugar at this point can be beneficial—will go a long way in preventing muscle breakdown.

And what about fats? In the post-workout period, you might want to go a bit easy on them. Fats slow down digestion. Normally, that's good, but post-HIT, you want to speed nutrients to your muscles as if your life depends on it. Because, in a way, it does—your HIT life, to be exact. And let's not forget hydration. Your body has just lost a significant amount of water through sweat. Dehydration, even slight, can set back recovery big time. So, don't be an idiot, chug that water like you've been lost in a desert.

A quick word about supplements: while they can be useful, they're the icing on the cake. Your primary focus should be whole, nutrient-dense foods. All the BCAAs, creatine, and other stuff are not a replacement for a well-structured pre and post-workout meal plan. Get the basics right before you even think about adding supplements to the mix.

It's a brutal truth, but one that needs to be said: you can't disconnect HIT from nutrition. That's like pulling the heart out of a living organism and expecting it to function. Your pre-workout nutrition primes you for the onslaught, and your post-workout nutrition is the repair crew, working tirelessly to rebuild the destruction you've just wrought. Fail in either of these, and you're not doing HIT; you're just going through motions, an actor on a stage with no audience, a king with no kingdom. So take control, seize the reins, and infuse your HIT with the nutritional strategy it demands. That's not a request; it's a damn necessity.

Individualism in Nutrition

You are a unique biochemical entity, not a cog in some nutritionist's grand wheel of sameness. If you believe that whatever worked for John or Jane Doe will work wonders for you too, then you're naïve or deluded, possibly both. The human body doesn't work like that. It never did and never will. And the sooner you grasp this fundamental truth, the better for your muscle gains, fat loss, and overall wellbeing. But if you're willing to gamble with your health and physique by following the herd, be my guest, but don't come crying when the cookie-cutter diet derails your progress and leaves you as average as ever.

Individualized nutrition is not a buzzword; it's a call to arms. We've been force-fed this idea that a bunch of generic principles can dictate how each of us should eat, move, and live. That's laughable. Our genetic makeup is so profoundly unique that even identical twins can react differently to the same diet. Have you ever considered the fact that your metabolic rate, your ability to process carbohydrates, your propensity to store fat, and even your psychological response to food are all elements governed by your own genetic code? Are you going to dismiss all that diversity and shove your round peg into a square hole? Because if you are, good luck with that strategy.

Food intolerances, nutrient absorption, hormonal fluctuations—they all conspire to make you a special snowflake in the avalanche that is human diversity. Let's talk food intolerances for a second. You think lactose intolerance is a fad? Or that gluten sensitivity is just for privileged folks with too much time to Google symptoms? If you're unable to process certain foods properly, your gut health can take a hit, and the cascade of problems that follow is anything but a joke. Inflammation, digestive distress, and nutrient deficiencies are just the tip of the iceberg. And you want to ignore all that because some nutrition guru says milk is excellent for everyone? That's not individualism; that's collective suicide.

Even the psychological elements of food can't be standardized. Some people can gorge on a cheat meal and bounce back effortlessly; others spiral into a bottomless pit of binge-eating. Some find solace in the comforting routine of set meals, while others need variety to keep their palate and soul satiated. And guess what? Both approaches are fine, as long as they align with your individual psychological make-up and lifestyle requirements. You can't standardize hunger any more than you can standardize ambition.

Now, what's all this building up to? It's leading to the most liberating, yet terrifying concept in nutrition: self-experimentation. You have to be both the scientist and the lab rat, painstakingly tweaking variables and observing results, all while acknowledging the possible placebo effect that your mind can play. You have to set aside your ego, your prejudices, and sometimes even your common sense, to discover what works for you. This could mean going against popular beliefs, enduring ridicule, and investing time and effort into something that might not pay off immediately.

Is your body more efficient at burning fat as fuel? Try a ketogenic diet. Do you feel lethargic without carbs? Maybe a balanced or carb-heavy diet is your alley. Do intermittent fasting if your lifestyle and natural hunger patterns align with it. Or split your meals if you find that more manageable. There's no right or wrong here, only what works for you and what doesn't. And how do you find that out? Not by listening to the pontificating 'experts' who claim to have solved the human nutritional puzzle, but by listening to your body, documenting how it responds to different food types, meal timings, and caloric levels.

Let's not kid ourselves; self-experimentation isn't for the faint-hearted. You'll face setbacks, and there will be times when you doubt the wisdom of straying from the beaten path. But here's the kicker: It's the only way to build a nutritional strategy that's tailor-made for you. Self-experimentation is not a destination; it's a ceaseless cycle of hypothesis, trial, error, and adaptation. But for those brave enough to embark on this individualistic quest, the rewards are priceless.

So, to recap—and yeah, I said I wouldn't do that, but bear with me—nutrition isn't democratic. It's not a matter of popular vote. Your body doesn't give a damn about the latest diet trends, nutritional pyramids, or what your gym buddy swears by. It listens to one voice and one voice only: Yours. So stop outsourcing your nutritional wisdom and start investing in the only diet plan that's worth a damn: the one built specifically for you, by you. Anything less is an exercise in futility and a disgrace to your individualistic essence.

The Key Elements

Amuscle-building diet is a sophisticated process that demands close attention to the ratios of macronutrients, the intake of micronutrients, and the overall balance of calories. The goal is to support muscle protein synthesis, fuel intense workouts, and promote overall health and recovery.

Protein is fundamental in any muscle-building diet. Its role in supporting muscle protein synthesis necessitates sufficient intake from a variety of sources, such as lean meats, poultry, fish, dairy products, and plant-based options like legumes. This ensures a broad spectrum of amino acids, essential for muscle repair and growth.

Carbohydrates are also vital, primarily in providing energy for demanding workouts and in replenishing glycogen stores in muscles. Choosing complex carbohydrates from sources like whole grains, fruits, and vegetables is beneficial for a sustained release of energy, helping to avoid energy dips during workouts.

Healthy fats, derived from sources like avocados, nuts, seeds, and olive oil, are crucial for hormone production and maintaining joint health. Balancing these macronutrients in proportion to individual goals and dietary needs is key to effective muscle building and overall health.

Micronutrients, often overlooked, play a significant role in bodybuilding diets. Vitamins and minerals, including vitamin D, calcium, magnesium, and iron, are essential for bone health, energy metabolism, and oxygen transport. Deficiencies in these nutrients can hinder muscle growth and athletic performance.

Hydration, crucial for muscle function and recovery, is an often-underestimated component of a muscle-building diet. Ensuring adequate fluid intake is essential for peak physical performance and post-exercise recovery.

Caloric intake must be aligned with the bodybuilder's goals, whether aiming for muscle gain or fat loss while preserving muscle mass. This requires a careful balance between consuming enough calories to support muscle growth and avoiding excessive calorie intake that can lead to fat accumulation.

Meal timing, especially around workouts, is critical for optimizing performance and recovery. Consuming the right nutrients before and after exercise can significantly impact energy levels during workouts and aid in muscle recovery afterward.

Regular assessments and dietary adjustments, ideally under professional guidance, are necessary to ensure that the nutrition plan remains aligned with the individual's evolving goals and needs. Tailoring a diet for muscle building involves a holistic approach, considering not just the physical demands of bodybuilding but also prioritizing overall health and well-being. This approach allows bodybuilders to achieve their physical goals while maintaining a healthy and sustainable lifestyle.

Hydration

Water is fundamental to maintaining a healthy, well-balanced diet, playing a critical role in a host of vital bodily functions. It constitutes a major portion of our body weight and is involved in essential processes such as the digestion of food, absorption of nutrients, and the transportation of key substances within the body.

Acting as a solvent, water enables chemical reactions, assists in regulating body temperature through mechanisms like sweating, and serves as a lubricant in joints. Its importance extends to cognitive health as well; even slight dehydration can impair focus and increase the sensation of tiredness, highlighting its role in mental performance.

Beyond cognitive function, water is key in eliminating waste products, thus aiding in maintaining kidney health and contributing to the health of the skin. For those involved in regular physical activity, the significance of water intake is even more pronounced. As exercise leads to fluid loss through perspiration, replenishing this fluid is crucial for sustaining hydration levels and avoiding dehydration.

The quantity of water required varies depending on factors such as an individual's age, sex, environmental conditions, and physical activity levels. A commonly suggested guideline is the intake of approximately eight 8-ounce glasses of water daily. This can be achieved through direct consumption of water or through the intake of hydrating foods, such as fruits and vegetables.

Neglecting proper hydration can lead to a variety of health complications, underscoring the importance of regular water intake for overall health. Prioritizing sufficient water consumption is a straightforward yet essential aspect of nutrition, pivotal for maintaining the body's overall health and wellness.

Protein

Protein stands as a vital element in nutrition, playing a key role in the formation, functioning, and regulation of the body's tissues and organs. It is composed of amino acids, the fundamental building blocks that drive numerous bodily processes. The body's inability to synthesize essential amino acids necessitates their acquisition through diet, highlighting the importance of protein in daily nutrition.

For those involved in physical activities or resistance training, the significance of protein is amplified. It is critical for the repair and growth of muscle tissue. Beyond muscle health, proteins are pivotal in synthesizing enzymes, hormones, and components of the immune system, thereby underpinning overall health and vitality.

Protein sources are varied, catering to a range of dietary needs and preferences. Animal-based proteins are found in lean meats like chicken, turkey, beef, and fish, along with dairy products such as milk, yogurt, and cheese. For those favoring plant-based diets, legumes, tofu, tempeh, beans, lentils, and protein-rich grains like quinoa are excellent options. Nuts and seeds offer not only protein but also essential fats and other key nutrients.

The amount of protein required daily can differ based on age, gender, level of physical activity, and specific health objectives. In general, consuming an adequate amount of protein is crucial for the body's growth, repair, and maintenance needs. Those who are physically active, including athletes, may find an increased protein intake beneficial for optimal muscle development and recovery.

Carbohydrates

Carbohydrates play a pivotal role in a balanced diet, acting as the primary and preferred energy source for bodily functions. Made up of sugars, starches, and fibers, they are metabolized into glucose, which is the fundamental fuel for cellular activities. This macronutrient is particularly crucial for those involved in regular physical activities and exercises due to its energy-providing capabilities.

Carbohydrates are categorized into two types: simple and complex. Simple carbohydrates, found in items like fruits, honey, and refined sugars, offer a rapid energy boost, but can also cause quick fluctuations in blood sugar levels. In contrast, complex carbohydrates, found in foods such as whole grains, legumes, vegetables, and fruits, provide energy more steadily, thanks to their slower digestion and absorption rates. Fiber, a component of complex carbohydrates, is vital for maintaining digestive health, aiding in satiety, and stabilizing blood sugar levels.

The recommended daily intake of carbohydrates varies and depends on individual factors like age, gender, physical activity level, and specific health objectives. A diet rich in complex carbohydrates, rather than simple sugars, is typically recommended for sustained energy and overall health. Foods like brown rice, quinoa, oats, and whole wheat, along with a variety of colorful fruits and vegetables, are not only excellent sources of carbohydrates but also provide essential vitamins, minerals, and fiber.

Fats

Fats are an indispensable part of a nutritious and balanced diet, offering a dense source of energy and playing various crucial roles in the body. Including fats in one's diet is key for overall health, but it's important to be mindful about the types and amounts of fats consumed.

Saturated fats are commonly found in animal products, such as meats and dairy, as well as in tropical oils like coconut and palm oil. While they are an important aspect of a balanced diet, it's advisable to consume them in moderation due to their potential impact on cardiovascular health. On the other hand, unsaturated fats, which include monounsaturated and polyunsaturated fats, offer significant health benefits. Monounsaturated fats, present in foods like olive oil, avocados, and nuts, are known for their heart-healthy properties and ability to help lower harmful cholesterol levels. Polyunsaturated fats, which encompass essential fatty acids such as Omega-3 and Omega-6, are vital for brain function and heart health. These can be found in fatty fish, flaxseeds, chia seeds, and walnuts. Trans fats, typically found in processed and fried foods, are associated with an increased risk of heart disease and should be limited in the diet.

Fats serve several essential functions in the body. They are stored in adipose tissue and act as a long-term energy reserve. Fats are also integral components of cell membranes, playing a crucial role in maintaining cell integrity and function. Additionally, they assist in the absorption of fat-soluble vitamins like A, D, E, and K.

A balanced diet should include a healthy intake of fats, focusing on unsaturated sources while limiting saturated and trans fats. Healthy fat sources like olive oil, avocados, nuts, seeds, and fatty fish are recommended. According to the American Heart Association, fats should constitute 20-35% of an individual's total daily calories, with the majority coming from unsaturated fats. The specific needs for fat intake can vary based on individual factors such as age, sex, activity level, and health conditions. Consulting with a healthcare professional or registered dietitian can help tailor one's fat intake to meet personal needs, ensuring a comprehensive and personalized approach to essential nutrition.

Micronutrients

Minerals and vitamins, as essential micronutrients, hold key roles in numerous physiological processes, contributing significantly to the overall health and functioning of the body. They are indispensable for a variety of functions including metabolism, immune system support, maintaining bone health, and preserving the health of skin, eyes, and other organs.

Minerals such as calcium are important for bone strength, muscle function, and blood clotting, with sources like dairy, leafy greens, and fortified foods. Iron, found in red meat, poultry, fish, beans, and fortified cereals, is crucial for the transport of oxygen in the blood. Magnesium, which plays a role in muscle and nerve function, blood sugar control, and bone health, is abundant in nuts, seeds, whole grains, and leafy greens. Potassium, necessary for heart and muscle function, can be found in bananas, potatoes, citrus fruits, and beans. Sodium, important for fluid balance and nerve function, is commonly found in table salt and various processed foods.

In the realm of vitamins, Vitamin A, found in carrots, sweet potatoes, spinach, and dairy, is essential for good vision, immune function, and skin health. Vitamin C, which is abundant in citrus fruits, berries, and bell peppers, aids in immune system support, wound healing, and collagen production. Vitamin D, crucial for bone health and immune function, can be obtained from sun exposure, fatty fish, and fortified foods. Vitamin E, an antioxidant that helps protect cells from damage, is found in nuts, seeds, and vegetable oils. Vitamin K, necessary for blood clotting and bone metabolism, is present in leafy greens, broccoli, and soybean oil.

To ensure adequate intake of these vital minerals and vitamins, a balanced and varied diet that includes fruits, vegetables, whole grains, lean proteins, and dairy or suitable alternatives is essential. Individual needs for these micronutrients can vary based on factors like age, gender, lifestyle, and specific health conditions. In certain situations, supplementation might be advisable. Consulting with healthcare professionals or dietitians can provide guidance on tailoring nutritional intake to meet individual requirements, ensuring a well-rounded and personalized approach to nutrition.

Simplicity and Efficiency

Striving for a chiseled physique with a six-pack, impressive biceps, and a V-shaped back often leads to an overzealous focus on every calorie, carb, and exercise. The tendency to micromanage has seeped into our approach to nutrition, and it's high time for a change. Nutrition, after all, isn't akin to quantum physics. There's no need to scrutinize every dietary decision to its minutest detail. What's needed instead is an appreciation for the elegance of simplicity and efficiency, and here's a guide on how to achieve that.

The concept of the 80/20 rule, or the Pareto Principle, is particularly relevant to nutrition. This principle suggests that 80% of your results can be attributed to 20% of your efforts. In other words, it's time to stop fretting over the minutiae. Is an extra slice of whole-grain toast going to derail your fitness goals? Unlikely. Yet, so many people get bogged down in such trivialities, wasting energy that could be better spent on more productive activities, like working out. The focus should be on the major factors that drive results—lean proteins, healthy fats, complex carbohydrates. These are the essentials that will contribute to the bulk of your fitness gains. And please, let go of the obsessive calorie counting. Set some basic guidelines, stick to them, and adjust as needed.

Moving on to meal prep, often seen as a daunting task that consumes an entire day. It doesn't have to be this way. Instead of a complex, multi-course menu, focus on mastering a few simple dishes that you can rotate throughout the week. Cook in bulk, simplify your choices, and streamline the cooking process. Remember, variety might be the spice of life, but when it comes to achieving specific fitness goals, simplicity reigns supreme. A simplified menu of nutrient-dense meals not only eases the burden of grocery shopping but also reduces preparation time.

Regarding grocery shopping, if you're spending more time browsing aisles than lifting weights, there's a problem. Approach grocery shopping with a plan. Make a list, adhere to it, and avoid getting sidetracked. There's no need to debate the merits of various brands or wander through every aisle. Focus on whole, unprocessed foods that pack the most nutritional value—lean meats, vegetables, fruits, nuts. These should be your staples, not the endless options of processed foods that can derail your diet. Efficient, smart shopping saves time and keeps you on track.

This principle of simplicity and efficiency isn't just for nutrition; it extends to all facets of life. Streamlining your diet frees up time and mental space for other important areas—your training, work, relationships. Efficiency in one aspect of life can create positive ripples in others. The time saved by not obsessing over insignificant food choices or lengthy grocery trips can be invested in workouts, deepening relationships, or personal growth.

Adopting a minimalist approach to your body doesn't mean hoarding; it means focusing on what's essential. Strip your nutrition down to the basics—the key principles that drive the most results. Embrace simplicity in your recipes, meal prep, and grocery habits. Life becomes less stressful when you're not constantly worried about your next meal or the exact macronutrient breakdown. Create a system, stick to it, and adjust as necessary. The 80/20 rule is more than a guideline; it's a way of life.

In a world that often complicates things unnecessarily, there's revolutionary power in simplicity and efficiency. Don't be ensnared by a complex system that drains more energy than it yields. Simplify your approach, focus on what's important, and watch as not just your nutrition, but your entire life transforms. You might start by streamlining your diet, but the real transformation is in how this simplicity permeates every aspect of your life. That's the real reward, the ultimate win, the game-changer. It's not just about what you eat; it's about enhancing your entire life.

Meal Planning and Preparation

I f you think meal planning is for the Martha Stewarts of the world, or that you can just wing it and still get jacked, you're selling yourself a stack of lies taller than a five-layer protein cake. Meal planning isn't some frou-frou activity you can skip; it's the strategic roadmap to your gains and fat loss. So, drop that doughnut and listen. If you aimlessly wander through your nutritional life, you're on a collision course with a mediocre physique and second-rate health. It's high time you toughen up and take control. No more excuses.

Let's talk about structuring your meals. How many times do you see people pulling their hair out over whether they should eat six small meals or three big ones? What they don't get is that there's no one-size-fits-all. Yeah, I know the 9-to-5 crowd loves the traditional three-square-meals-a-day model. But if you're hitting the iron temple hard, you may find that five or six smaller meals keep your energy steady and help you recover better. Experiment. Fine-tune. Adapt. And for heaven's sake, don't get entangled in dogma. Your meal structure should be as unique as your fingerprint; it should serve your life, your goals, and your workout schedule. Stop looking for a meal plan to copy and paste into your life. Instead, create a template that bends to your will. Keep the basics consistent: a solid source of protein, a helping of veggies, some quality fats, and smart carbs. The ratios might vary depending on whether you're bulking, cutting, or maintaining, but the fundamental structure remains the same.

That said, let's shatter another myth: every meal doesn't have to be a gourmet feast. You're fueling your body, not auditioning for a cooking show. The quicker you get this, the easier your life will become. Get a list of foods that work for you. A list so damn fine-tuned that you could shop for it in your sleep. What's that? You hate cooking? No one's asking you to be a Michelin-star chef. But you do have to get into the kitchen and actually prepare your food. Think assembly line, not art studio. Have your protein sources—chicken, fish, beef, whatever—prepped and ready to go. Cook them in batches, freeze what you won't use immediately, and refrigerate the rest. Same with veggies. Cut them up, toss them in some olive oil, and roast a massive sheet of them. Store them in airtight containers. When it's time to eat, it's as simple as mix and match.

While we're talking preparation, let's discuss the sanctity of the Sunday meal prep. Some of you worship this ritual like it's some sort of sacred ceremony. Let's get real. You don't need to give up your entire Sunday to set yourself up for the week. With some strategic multitasking, you can cut that time in half or even less. Got a pressure cooker or an Instant Pot? Use it to cook large batches of protein while you chop your veggies. While those are cooking, you can portion out your snacks for the week—nuts, fruits, whatever floats your boat. By the time your proteins are cooked, you'll be halfway done. And no, you don't need to put every meal into separate, Instagram-worthy containers. Store foods in larger containers and portion them out as needed. Unless you're some kind of social media influencer trying to impress your followers, no one cares if your meals are aesthetically displayed. Get it cooked, get it stored, get on with your life.

Now, about adaptability. Your well-crafted meal plan isn't a prison. Life happens. Maybe you're stuck in traffic, or perhaps a last-minute work crisis keeps you late at the office. What then? You adapt, that's what. Keep some non-perishable, healthy snacks in your car or at your desk. I'm talking about foods that won't spoil—protein bars that aren't loaded with sugar, small packets of almonds, and so on. You may not get your meticulously planned grilled chicken salad, but you won't spiral into dietary anarchy either. Sometimes you have to pivot, and that's okay. Adaptability doesn't mean weakness; it means you're resilient and versatile. Keep the core tenets of your nutritional philosophy in mind, and you can make any situation work in your favor.

Look, food is fuel, and meal planning is the logistics of how you're going to get that fuel into the tank. But remember this: the most advanced fighter jet is useless if it's not refueled properly and on time. You can't afford to leave your nutrition to chance, not if you're serious about your goals. Your meals should be as dialed-in as your workouts, planned with military precision yet flexible enough to adapt to life's curveballs. This isn't rocket science; it's logic. It's the marriage of strategy and tactics, the intersection where foresight meets execution. With the right plan and preparation, you're not just feeding your body; you're forging it. And don't even get me started on those who say it's too hard or too time-consuming. If you have time to binge-watch a Netflix series or scroll aimlessly through social media, you have time to plan and prep your meals.

The path to peak performance is not filled with shortcuts or built on haphazard decisions. No, it's created by diligent, calculated planning and relentless execution. So, stop treating meal planning like it's some kind of afterthought or a chore to be avoided. It's neither. It's a tool—a powerful, game-changing tool that will catapult you closer to your fitness goals at warp speed. Ignore it at your peril. Embrace it and become a master of your own fate. It's your call. Make it a good one.

Foods and Meals

What would a meal plan inspired by Mentzer look like? Protein would take center stage, of course. Not the watered-down, overly processed garbage you find in the aisles of your local grocery store but robust, real sources like lean cuts of beef, chicken, fish, and perhaps even some plant-based alternatives like tempeh or seitan for those who swing that way. You'd prepare these in the most straightforward, no-nonsense manner, such as grilling or roasting, shunning excessive oils and unnecessary sauces. Seasonings would be simple—salt, pepper, perhaps some garlic and herbs. Why? Because when you're training at the intensity Mentzer advocated, you don't need to drown your tastebuds; you need to fuel the beast within.

Pre and post-workout meals would certainly include complex carbohydrates like brown rice, quinoa, or sweet potatoes to refuel glycogen stores and to prep the body for the high-intensity torture you're about to unleash on it. No sugary cereals, no white bread, and definitely no candy bars. It's about functional nutrition, purpose-driven eating where each morsel serves a role in the greater strategy of your physique and performance goals.

As for fats, Mentzer would advocate for the healthy kinds found in avocados, nuts, and olive oil, keeping a keen eye on caloric content because let's be real—fats are calorie-dense, and you can't afford unnecessary baggage when you're striving for optimal performance and body composition. For Mentzer, excess body fat would be seen as nothing but dead weight, something to be eradicated as ruthlessly as a weak mindset or a lack of training intensity. So, when it comes to fats, you're not gorging on them; you're strategically incorporating them to maximize hormone production, brain function, and satiety.

Now, on to meal timing. Mentzer wouldn't have been caught dead snacking on empty-calorie trash, so why should you? Each meal would be a carefully timed event, designed to provide maximum sustenance and nutritional value. You eat when you need to eat, not when society tells you it's time for a break. Is your body genuinely screaming for fuel at 11 a.m., or are you just bored at work? If Mentzer wouldn't put up with weak, aimless snacking behavior, neither should you. Listen to your body, not the clock on the wall or the pangs of mindless habit.

Mentzer would have been all about supplementation but only if it made logical sense. So yes, a quality protein supplement could find its way into your diet, but only if your daily protein needs weren't being met through whole foods. Would he go for the flashiest supplement with the most Instagram followers? Not a chance. He'd go for something with a solid amino acid profile, free of unnecessary fillers and sweeteners. As for other supplements, a multivitamin might get a pass, perhaps some fish oil, and maybe even creatine monohydrate given its well-researched benefits on high-intensity performance.

Let's not forget hydration. You think Mentzer would be caught dead sipping on sugary sodas or artificial juices? Hell no. Water would be the go-to, with the occasional foray into electrolyte-enhanced beverages, particularly after grueling, sweat-drenched workouts. Because when you're training at the level of intensity that Mentzer preached, dehydration is not an option. You hydrate to dominate, to prepare your body for the next onslaught of high-intensity mayhem.

Now, for those who think a Mentzer-inspired meal plan would involve endless hours slaving away in the kitchen—think again. The man was about efficiency in all things, and your meal prep would be no different. You'd cook in bulk, maximizing your time and effort. Your meals would be straightforward, devoid of unnecessary culinary flair. Every chop, every sizzle, every seasoning shake would serve a singular purpose:

to fuel your next high-intensity workout and to optimize your recovery.

And let's put to rest the notion that Mentzer would endorse any kind of one-size-fits-all meal plan. The man was an advocate for individualized approaches in training, and this would extend to nutrition. What works for one person might not work for another, and Mentzer would be the first to tell you to spend some time identifying the unique set of nutritional variables that propel you towards your goals most efficiently.

So when you sit down to craft your Mike Mentzer-inspired meal plan, remember that you're not just shoving food into a hole in your face; you're engaging in an act of defiance against mediocrity, against the legions of fitness phonies who think that optimum body composition can be achieved through shortcuts and gimmicks. You're embodying the spirit of a man who never settled for second-best, who lived and breathed the principles of intensity, efficiency, and individualized, science-based strategy. Your nutrition isn't just a footnote to your training; it's an integral part of a holistic approach to achieving a jaw-dropping physique and unparalleled performance. So go ahead, plan your meals with the ferocity and attention to detail that Mentzer would demand, and then execute that plan with a single-minded focus that would make even him nod in approval. Anything less is an insult to the legacy of a man who took no prisoners in his relentless pursuit of bodybuilding perfection.

The Role of Supplements

When do you actually need to reach for that supplement bottle? You reach for it when your diet falls short, when the demands of your high-intensity training sessions outstrip the nutrients you can obtain from whole foods. There's no supplement on the market that's going to replace the fundamental building blocks you get from quality protein, complex carbohydrates, and essential fats. Don't kid yourself; if your nutritional foundation is shaky, no amount of supplementation will make up for it.

Here's another bit of real talk: If you're busting your backside in the gym and meticulously monitoring your nutritional intake, certain supplements can aid in recovery and performance. That's not an endorsement to run out and bankrupt yourself buying everything that says "performance-enhancing" on the bottle. We're talking about targeted supplementation that complements your diet and training regimen, not replaces it.

Let's talk protein powder. It's the bread and butter of the supplement world, and for good reason. The gym is where you break down muscle fibers, but it's protein that builds them back up stronger. Can you get enough from food? Absolutely. But let's be real: Preparing and consuming vast amounts of animal or plant protein is not always practical. A quality protein powder—whether it's whey, casein, or a plant-based option—can plug those gaps, especially when you're on the go or immediately post-workout when convenience is crucial.

Now, creatine monohydrate—arguably the most researched supplement on the market. If you're engaging in high-intensity, short-duration activities, this is a supplement you can't afford to overlook. Multiple studies show its ability to increase power output and muscular endurance, which translates into more effective training sessions. If you think this is for the bodybuilding elite, you're wrong. The benefits are universal, from gym newbies to seasoned veterans. But stay smart—buy pure, unadulterated creatine monohydrate. No need for the flashy versions with additives that hike up the price and deliver nothing extra.

Caffeine is another tool in your supplement arsenal. The pre-workout market is flooded with products that have caffeine as a main ingredient, often mixed with a cocktail of other questionable components. But guess what? You don't need that garbage. Pure caffeine—whether from a pill or a cup of black coffee—is enough to give you that kick, to heighten alertness and reduce the perception of effort during exercise. But moderation is key; the aim is heightened performance, not a racing heartbeat and jittery hands.

Then there are branched-chain amino acids (BCAAs), which are often touted as the holy grail for muscle recovery. The hard truth? If you're getting sufficient protein, you probably don't need them. However, if you train fasted or see that your diet lacks quality protein sources, BCAAs can offer some benefit in terms of muscle recovery and performance.

Fish oil and multivitamins fall under what could be considered 'health insurance' supplements. Omega-3 fatty acids found in fish oil have a range of benefits, from anti-inflammatory properties to cognitive function improvement. Most modern diets are high in Omega-6 and low in Omega-3, so supplementing can restore that balance. A quality multivitamin can act as a nutritional safety net but is not an excuse for a poor diet. They're not a get-out-of-jail-free card that allows you to eat garbage. They're there to cover your bases, nothing more.

You want a dose of reality? Supplements aren't magic; they're tools. They can optimize your training and plug gaps in your nutrition, but they won't make up for a lackluster training regimen or a subpar diet. Stop looking for easy solutions in a bottle and start focusing on what matters—consistent, high-intensity training and a diet built on real, whole foods. Anything less is a slap in the face to anyone serious about their physical performance and overall health. There's no shortcut, no magic pill, and no supplement that will do the work for you. So the next time you're drawn by the allure of flashy supplement marketing, remind yourself: The only thing you should be loading up on is a heavy dose of self-discipline and unyielding dedication to your training and nutrition. Supplements are the sidekick, not the hero of your fitness narrative. Make no mistake about it; relying on them as your main source of hope is as misguided as expecting a pocket knife to win a war. They're an adjunct, an add-on, a tactical resource in a broader strategy aimed at maximizing your physical potential. So use them wisely, or not at all.

Common Misconceptions

Get ready to have your notions shattered and myths dismantled. Strap in, because the next few minutes of your life are going to be a gut punch to all those misconceptions you've been holding dear. First on the chopping block: the Anabolic Window, that magical period after your workout where you're led to believe your muscles are gaping maws, starving for protein and carbs. How many of you have bolted from the gym straight to your shaker bottle, worried that a minute's delay will result in catastrophic muscle loss? Let's break it down. The idea behind the Anabolic Window is that post-exercise, there's an acute period where nutrient uptake is optimized, and failure to feed the muscles during this time will result in less-than-optimal gains. Research does show increased muscle protein synthesis post-workout, but here's where the half-truths start to spread. That window isn't a fleeting 30 minutes; it extends for several hours. In fact, if you've had a protein-rich meal a few hours before working out, your body is still utilizing those nutrients for recovery. The takeaway? Stop treating the post-workout period like a ticking time bomb.

Now, let's rip apart another darling of the fitness industry: the doctrine of small, frequent meals to "stoke the metabolic fire." The idea here is that eating every 2-3 hours boosts your metabolism, keeps the fat-burning furnace humming, and provides a steady stream of nutrients to your muscles. Sounds logical, right? Except it's not. The thermic effect of food, which is the energy your body expends to digest, absorb, and dispose of nutrients, is directly proportional to the caloric content of the meal. Whether you eat three 800-calorie meals or six 400-calorie meals, the thermic effect remains constant. So why has this myth persisted? In part, it's because frequent meals can help manage hunger and blood sugar levels. But let's be clear: that's a far cry from saying it accelerates fat loss or muscle gain. Furthermore, the hassle of prepping, packing, and eating six meals a day can add unnecessary stress, making it an impractical approach for many people.

Then there's the nebulous concept of 'Clean Eating,' a phrase that's been twisted, contorted, and overused to the point of being rendered meaningless. No one can even agree on what 'clean' means. Is it organic? Is it whole foods? Is it gluten-free, dairy-free, joy-free? Here's the issue: food isn't clean or dirty; it's a spectrum of nutritional choices that should align with both your health goals and your enjoyment of life. Categorizing foods into these binary definitions creates unhealthy relationships with eating. What's often ignored in the clean eating dialogue is the concept of nutrient density versus caloric content. A piece of salmon might be calorically dense, but it's also nutrient-rich, providing essential fatty acids, high-quality protein, and various vitamins. A bowl of organic, gluten-free cereal might be championed as 'clean,' but if it's void of essential nutrients, how beneficial is it really? Another pitfall of the 'clean eating' mantra is the unspoken implication that anything that falls outside of this arbitrary category is 'dirty' and, therefore, off-limits. This black-and-white mentality ignores the fact that moderation is key and that a well-balanced diet can and should include a variety of foods.

So why do these myths persist? Because they're convenient narratives that package complex nutritional science into neat, marketable concepts. These myths are perpetuated by influencers, fitness gurus, and even well-intentioned gym buddies, but they don't hold up under scrutiny. They simplify the multi-faceted relationship between food, body composition, and performance into a few easily digestible soundbites that people can latch onto without having to delve into the nitty-gritty details. But guess what? Biology doesn't care about convenience. Your body doesn't operate based on catchy phrases or trendy diets. It operates on the laws of thermodynamics, biochemistry, and physiology. So stop falling for these simplified concepts that only serve to make your relationship with nutrition more complicated than it needs to be.

The reality of nutrition is that it's a complex interplay of variables: macronutrient ratios, caloric intake, activity levels, hormonal balance, and a dozen other factors that no single dietary regimen can fully encapsulate. It's not enough to follow a dietary dogma blindly; you must understand the 'why' behind your choices. Strip away the myths, and what you're left with is the raw truth: effective nutrition is based on science, not slogans. It's grounded in an understanding of how nutrients fuel physical processes, how our bodies assimilate and utilize what we consume, and how different foods can affect our metabolic rate, our mood, and even our cognitive functions. Armed with that knowledge, you can navigate the complexities of nutrition, make informed choices, and ultimately, get one step closer to your ideal physique or performance level. Forget the myths. Focus on the facts. And for heaven's sake, don't let another day pass living under the tyranny of these misconceptions. Your body deserves better.

Overview of the Training Philosophy

M ike Mentzer's Heavy Duty training system revolutionized bodybuilding with its high-intensity training (HIT) approach, significantly impacting the sport even decades after its introduction. This system, heavily influenced by Arthur Jones' HIT philosophy, was Mentzer's unique interpretation and expansion into a more radical regimen. Mentzer's philosophy was not just about lifting weights; it was a holistic approach encompassing training, nutrition, and mindset, tailored for both professional bodybuilders and average, drug-free individuals striving for their natural muscular potential.

The cornerstone of Mentzer's training philosophy was intensity. He defined intensity as "the percentage of possible momentary muscular effort being exerted," emphasizing the need to push muscles to their absolute limit. For Mentzer, the key to muscle hypertrophy was not the volume of exercise but the intensity. He believed in reaching as close to 100% exertion as possible during reps to stimulate muscle growth. This approach was corroborated by scientific research, which highlighted the role of mechanical tension in muscle growth. Mentzer's description of the "last rep" showcases his philosophy vividly - the final, nearly impossible repetition, full of exertion, was seen as crucial in triggering the body's muscle growth mechanisms.

To achieve this high level of intensity, Mentzer incorporated techniques like pre-exhausting muscle groups, assisted lifting, and holding weights at different points during the lift. These methods were designed to bring the bodybuilder closer to muscle failure more quickly, thus maximizing muscle growth potential. The emphasis was on reaching failure with each exercise, a principle central to the Heavy Duty method.

Another pivotal aspect of Mentzer's philosophy was low workout volume. He argued against the then-prevailing notion that more volume in weight training was better. Instead, Mentzer suggested a low volume approach, emphasizing that fewer reps with heavier weight could achieve the necessary intensity for muscle growth more effectively than numerous reps with lighter weight. This approach was not just about efficiency in training; it also allowed bodybuilders time for other pursuits, like studying or art, reflecting Mentzer's holistic view of bodybuilding as part of a balanced life. Initially, Mentzer prescribed 1 to 2 sets of 6 to 8 reps for each exercise, performed to failure. The goal was to increase the weight by 10% once 12 reps could be achieved in a set, thus maintaining the challenge and intensity.

Mentzer also stressed the importance of low frequency in workouts. He believed that recovery was crucial since muscles grow from the stimulus of weightlifting during the recovery phase. In his most extreme version of Heavy Duty, he recommended performing 1 to 2 sets for a muscle group just once a week, allowing the other six days for recovery. This perspective was rooted in the understanding that recovery is as essential as the workout itself for muscle growth. The idea was to provide enough stimulus during the workout to promote growth, but then to allow ample time for the body to recover and adapt.

Mike Mentzer's training philosophy, epitomized by his Heavy Duty system, represented a significant shift from traditional bodybuilding methods. It emphasized the quality of the workout over quantity, focusing on intensity, low volume, and sufficient recovery. This approach was tailored to maximize muscle growth in the most efficient and effective way possible, challenging the conventional wisdom of the bodybuilding world at the time. Mentzer's legacy continues through the athletes and trainers who adopt and adapt his principles, proving the enduring impact of his revolutionary ideas on the world of bodybuilding.

The Mentzer Method

Mike Mentzer was not a man of few words when it came to training, and his method reflects this directness and simplicity. In this chapter, we will delve into the core principles of the Mentzer Method, often referred to as High-Intensity Training or HIT. Mike Mentzer's approach to bodybuilding and strength training was rooted in science, logic, and a fierce determination to maximize results while minimizing wasted effort.

At its core, the Mentzer Method is about efficiency and intensity. Unlike the endless hours some spend at the gym, Mentzer advocated for short, intense workouts that leave no room for half-hearted efforts. This no-nonsense approach was a stark contrast to the prevailing wisdom of his time, which often advocated high volume and frequent training sessions.

Mentzer's journey into the world of bodybuilding began with a fascination for the human body's capacity for growth and adaptation. He was not content with merely following the crowd; he sought to understand the underlying mechanisms that drive muscle growth and strength development. This quest for knowledge led him to develop the Mentzer Method, a revolutionary approach that challenges many of the conventional beliefs about training.

One of the foundational principles of the Mentzer Method is the concept of intensity. Mike Mentzer believed that it was not the quantity of training that mattered, but the quality. He argued that by pushing your muscles to their limits in a brief, focused workout, you could stimulate significant growth and strength gains. This meant lifting heavier weights, performing fewer repetitions, and training to absolute failure.

In a world where some individuals spent hours lifting weights without ever truly challenging themselves, Mentzer's approach was a wake-up call. He believed that true growth came from pushing your muscles beyond their comfort zone, where they had no choice but to adapt and become stronger. This approach wasn't for the faint of heart; it demanded mental fortitude and unwavering commitment.

Mike Mentzer's training philosophy also emphasized the importance of progressive overload. This means consistently increasing the resistance or intensity of your workouts over time. Without this progressive challenge, your muscles have no reason to grow. Mentzer saw many individuals stagnate in their training because they failed to increase the demands on their muscles.

To implement progressive overload effectively, Mentzer developed a system of tracking and monitoring your progress. This involved meticulous record-keeping of every workout, including the weight lifted, number of repetitions, and any changes in performance. This data-driven approach allowed individuals to ensure that they were continually pushing the envelope and making gains.

Another crucial aspect of the Mentzer Method is the principle of brief, infrequent workouts. Mentzer believed that extended training sessions were counterproductive, as they could lead to overtraining and burnout. Instead, he recommended short and intense workouts that focused on compound exercises and targeted all major muscle groups.

Mentzer's workouts were designed to be highly efficient, targeting multiple muscle groups simultaneously. This meant exercises like squats, deadlifts, bench presses, and rows took center stage in his routines. By engaging multiple muscles at once, these compound movements allowed for maximum stimulation in minimal time.

However, the intensity of these workouts cannot be overstated. The Mentzer Method required individuals to push themselves to the brink of failure, where they could no longer complete another repetition with proper form. This point of muscular failure was not just a suggestion; it was a non-negotiable part of the training process.

One of the most controversial aspects of Mike Mentzer's philosophy was his approach to training frequency. Unlike the conventional wisdom of the time, which often advocated for training each muscle group multiple times a week, Mentzer promoted infrequent training. He argued that muscles needed ample time to recover and grow between workouts.

Mentzer typically recommended training each muscle group only once a week. This allowed for maximum recovery and growth while minimizing the risk of overtraining. However, it also meant that each workout had to be brutally intense to stimulate sufficient growth during that single session.

To some, this approach seemed counterintuitive. After all, wouldn't more frequent training lead to faster results? Mentzer believed otherwise. He asserted that it was the quality of training that mattered most, not the quantity. By training infrequently but with extreme intensity, individuals could achieve remarkable results without overtaxing their bodies.

The Mentzer Method also placed a significant emphasis on rest and recovery. Mike Mentzer recognized that muscle growth occurred during the periods of rest between workouts, not during the actual training sessions. Without adequate rest, the body could not repair and rebuild muscle tissue effectively.

Rest days were not considered a sign of weakness in the Mentzer Method but a vital component of the training process. In fact, Mentzer often advised individuals to take as much rest as necessary between workouts to ensure full recovery. This might mean having several days of rest between training sessions for a specific muscle group.

Nutrition played a critical role in Mike Mentzer's approach to bodybuilding. He understood that proper nutrition was essential to support muscle growth and recovery. Without the right nutrients, even the most intense training sessions would yield subpar results.

Mentzer advocated for a high-protein diet to ensure an adequate supply of amino acids, the building blocks of muscle tissue. Protein was considered the cornerstone of a bodybuilder's diet, and he recommended consuming protein-rich foods such as lean meats, eggs, and dairy products.

Carbohydrates were also a vital component of the diet, providing the energy necessary for intense workouts. However, Mentzer advised controlling carbohydrate intake to prevent excessive fat gain. He suggested focusing on complex carbohydrates like whole grains and vegetables while minimizing simple sugars.

Fat intake was not demonized in the Mentzer Method. In fact, Mentzer believed that healthy fats were essential for hormone production and overall health. He recommended sources of healthy fats like avocados, nuts, and olive oil.

To complement their diets, many individuals following the Mentzer Method also used supplements. Protein supplements, such as whey protein, were common additions to ensure sufficient protein intake. Creatine, a supplement known for enhancing strength and performance, was also popular among Mentzer's followers.

Understanding macronutrients and micronutrients was a fundamental aspect of the Mentzer Method. Mike Mentzer stressed the importance of knowing what you were putting into your body and how it would support your training goals. This knowledge allowed individuals to tailor their diets to their specific needs and goals.

In addition to nutrition, Mike Mentzer recognized the importance of mental strength in achieving success in bodybuilding and strength training. He believed that a strong mind was just as crucial as a strong body. Mentzer often spoke about the mental aspects of training, emphasizing the need for unwavering commitment and focus.

Setting realistic goals was a key element of Mentzer's approach to mental strength. He believed that individuals should have clear, achievable objectives in their training. These goals served as motivators and provided a sense of direction. Without specific goals, training could become aimless and ineffective.

However, achieving these goals often required individuals to push themselves beyond their perceived limits. Mentzer was a firm believer in the power of pushing through mental barriers. He encouraged individuals to embrace discomfort and to see it as a sign of progress.

Overcoming plateaus was a common challenge in bodybuilding and strength training, and Mentzer had strategies to address this issue. He believed that plateaus were often the result of individuals becoming too comfortable in their routines. To break through plateaus, he recommended implementing changes in training variables, such as increasing weights, altering rep ranges, or introducing new exercises.

Mindset and Motivation

Mike Mentzer was a man who understood that the battle in the gym was not just physical; it was mental. In this chapter, we will explore the crucial role that mindset and motivation played in Mike Mentzer's training philosophy. His approach went beyond the weights and sets; it delved into the inner workings of the human psyche, emphasizing the importance of mental strength and motivation.

Mentzer believed that the mind was the driving force behind any successful training regimen. Without the right mindset, even the most meticulously crafted workout plans would fall flat. He often said, "The body achieves what the mind believes," and this mantra encapsulated his philosophy.

One of the central tenets of Mike Mentzer's mindset philosophy was setting realistic goals. He didn't believe in vague aspirations or lofty dreams without a concrete plan. Instead, he advocated for specific, achievable objectives that could be measured and tracked.

Setting realistic goals served multiple purposes. First, it provided a clear target to work towards, giving training a sense of purpose and direction. Second, it allowed for the measurement of progress. Mentzer was a staunch advocate of data-driven training, and having clear goals enabled individuals to track their advancements or setbacks.

But setting goals wasn't enough; Mentzer emphasized the importance of commitment to those goals. He believed that success in bodybuilding and strength training required unwavering dedication. This wasn't about casually pursuing fitness; it was about making a pact with yourself and sticking to it no matter what.

Mentzer often compared the pursuit of physical excellence to a battle, and he expected individuals to approach it with the same determination and resolve as a soldier going to war. He believed that the mental fortitude to persevere through discomfort and adversity was the hallmark of a true champion.

Overcoming plateaus was another area where mindset played a pivotal role in Mentzer's philosophy. Plateaus were inevitable in any training journey, but how individuals dealt with them made all the difference. Mentzer saw plateaus not as roadblocks but as opportunities for growth.

His approach to breaking through plateaus was simple but effective: change something. Whether it was increasing the weight lifted, altering rep ranges, or introducing new exercises, Mentzer believed that complacency was the enemy of progress. He encouraged individuals to view plateaus as challenges to be conquered rather than reasons to give up.

A key aspect of Mike Mentzer's mindset philosophy was the acceptance of discomfort. He didn't sugarcoat the reality of intense training; it was hard, it was painful, and it pushed you to your limits. But he believed that it was precisely in those moments of discomfort that true growth occurred.

Mentzer's philosophy was a stark contrast to the prevailing notion that exercise should always be enjoyable and comfortable. He argued that the comfort zone was where mediocrity thrived, and true progress lay just beyond its borders. To reach new heights, individuals needed to embrace the discomfort of pushing their bodies to the limit.

In essence, Mentzer encouraged individuals to develop mental toughness. He believed that mental strength was as trainable as physical strength and that it could be honed through consistent, challenging workouts. It wasn't a trait reserved for a select few; it was a skill that anyone could develop with dedication and practice.

Another crucial element of Mentzer's mindset philosophy was the concept of failure. He didn't see failure as something to be feared or avoided; instead, he viewed it as a necessary stepping stone to success. Failure in the gym was not a sign of weakness but a badge of honor, indicating that you had pushed yourself to your limits.

Mentzer's approach to failure was uncompromising. He believed in training to absolute muscle failure, where you couldn't perform another repetition with proper form. This was the point where growth was stimulated, where the body was forced to adapt and become stronger.

But Mentzer also saw failure as a teacher. It provided valuable feedback on your performance and highlighted areas that needed improvement. Instead of shying away from failure, he encouraged individuals to embrace it, learn from it, and use it as a catalyst for future progress.

One of the significant challenges individuals faced in their training journey was staying motivated. Motivation could wane over time, especially when faced with the rigors of intense training and the inevitable setbacks that came with it. Mentzer had a straightforward solution: find your why.

He believed that everyone had a deep, personal reason for wanting to improve their physique or strength. Whether it was a desire to be healthier, to gain confidence, or to prove something to oneself, that underlying motivation was a powerful force.

Mentzer encouraged individuals to dig deep and uncover their true reasons for training. Once they identified their why, it became a wellspring of motivation that could fuel their workouts even on the toughest days. It was a reminder of their purpose and the driving force behind their commitment.

But motivation wasn't something that could be relied upon solely from within. Mentzer also emphasized the importance of external motivation, whether it came from a training partner, a coach, or a support system. Having someone to share the journey with and hold you accountable could make a world of difference in staying motivated.

Mentzer's approach to motivation was not about fleeting inspiration or quick fixes. He saw it as a long-term, sustainable force that would carry individuals through their entire training journey. It required dedication, self-reflection, and a deep connection to one's goals.

Mike Mentzer's training philosophy was not for the faint of heart. It demanded mental strength and unwavering commitment. It required individuals to set clear, achievable goals, embrace discomfort, and view failure as a stepping stone to success. It called for a level of motivation that went beyond surface-level inspiration and tapped into the deeper reasons for training.

Workout Routines

M ike Mentzer's approach to workout routines was a sharp departure from the conventional wisdom of his time. He didn't believe in long hours spent in the gym, mindlessly going through the motions. Instead, he advocated for short, intense workouts that left no room for mediocrity. In this chapter, we'll delve into the nitty-gritty of the workout routines that formed the core of the Mentzer Method.

At the heart of Mentzer's training philosophy was the principle of high-intensity training, often referred to as HIT. This approach was a stark contrast to the high-volume training regimens that were prevalent in the bodybuilding world. Instead of endless sets and repetitions, Mentzer's workouts were characterized by brief, focused sessions that pushed muscles to their limits.

The key to high-intensity training was, as the name suggests, intensity. Mentzer believed that the quality of training was far more critical than the quantity. It wasn't about how much time you spent in the gym; it was about how hard you worked during that time. Every set, every repetition, had to be a testament to your commitment and effort.

Mentzer's workouts were not for the faint of heart. They demanded a level of intensity that left individuals breathless, drenched in sweat, and on the verge of muscle failure. This was not a casual stroll through the gym; it was a full-blown battle with the iron.

Central to Mentzer's workout routines were compound exercises. These were multi-joint movements that engaged multiple muscle groups simultaneously. Exercises like squats, deadlifts, bench presses, and rows took center stage in his training programs.

Compound exercises were the backbone of Mentzer's approach for several reasons. First, they allowed for maximum muscle recruitment, ensuring that no potential for growth was left untapped. Second, they were highly efficient, targeting multiple muscle groups in a single movement. This efficiency was critical in keeping workouts short and intense.

Intensity was not a vague concept in the Mentzer Method; it was quantifiable. Mentzer believed in training to absolute muscle failure, the point at which you could no longer complete another repetition with proper form.

This was the point where true growth was stimulated, where the body had no choice but to adapt and become stronger.

To achieve this level of intensity, Mentzer employed techniques like forced repetitions and negatives. Forced repetitions involved having a spotter assist you in completing additional reps beyond the point of failure. Negatives, on the other hand, focused on the eccentric phase of the movement, where you resisted the weight's descent.

These advanced techniques were not for beginners but were tools that could be employed by experienced lifters looking to push their limits further. They added an extra layer of intensity to workouts, taking individuals to the brink of their physical capabilities.

Workout frequency was another aspect of the Mentzer Method that challenged conventional wisdom. While many advocated for training each muscle group multiple times a week, Mentzer recommended a different approach: infrequent, but intensely focused training.

He typically advised training each muscle group only once a week. This seemingly low frequency raised eyebrows, but Mentzer had a rationale behind it. He believed that muscles needed ample time to recover and grow between workouts. Overtraining, in his view, was a prevalent issue that hindered progress.

However, infrequent training did not mean easy training. Quite the opposite; it meant that each workout had to be brutally intense to stimulate sufficient growth during that single session. There was no room for half-hearted efforts or excuses. It was all or nothing.

Workout structure in the Mentzer Method was straightforward yet effective. A typical routine would involve a few compound exercises targeting all major muscle groups. These exercises would be performed with maximum effort, often to the point of failure. The brevity of the workout was compensated for by its intensity.

Rest periods between sets were kept minimal. The goal was to maintain an elevated heart rate and keep the muscles under tension. This approach not only saved time but also contributed to the overall intensity of the workout. There was no time for idle chit-chat or distractions in a Mentzer-style training session.

Mentzer's approach to workout routines also emphasized the importance of tracking and monitoring progress. He was a firm believer in data-driven training, and he expected individuals to keep meticulous records of every workout. This included details like the weight lifted, the number of repetitions, and any changes in performance.

These records served multiple purposes. First and foremost, they allowed individuals to ensure that they were continually pushing themselves to their limits.

Progress was not a vague concept; it was a tangible, measurable result of their efforts. Stagnation was not an option when armed with this data.

Second, tracking progress helped in making informed adjustments to workout routines. If an individual noticed that a particular exercise or muscle group was not progressing as desired, they could make targeted changes to address the issue. This data-driven approach ensured that workouts remained effective and efficient.

In addition to tracking progress, Mentzer encouraged individuals to embrace a holistic view of their training. This meant considering factors beyond the gym, such as nutrition, rest, and recovery. Training was just one piece of the puzzle; the other pieces had to fit together seamlessly for optimal results.

Rest and recovery played a critical role in the Mentzer Method. Mentzer understood that muscle growth and adaptation occurred during periods of rest, not during the actual training sessions. Without adequate rest, the body could not repair and rebuild muscle tissue effectively.

Rest days were not considered a sign of weakness in the Mentzer Method but a vital component of the training process. In fact, Mentzer often advised individuals to take as much rest as necessary between workouts to ensure full recovery. This might mean having several days of rest between training sessions for a specific muscle group.

Nutrition was another cornerstone of Mike Mentzer's approach to bodybuilding and strength training. He believed that proper nutrition was essential to support muscle growth and recovery. Without the right nutrients, even the most intense training sessions would yield subpar results.

Protein intake was a focal point of the diet in the Mentzer Method. Protein provided the essential amino acids necessary for muscle repair and growth. Mentzer recommended consuming protein-rich foods like lean meats, eggs, and dairy products to ensure an adequate supply.

Carbohydrates were also an integral part of the diet, providing the energy needed for intense workouts. However, Mentzer advised controlling carbohydrate intake to prevent excessive fat gain. He suggested focusing on complex carbohydrates like whole grains and vegetables while minimizing simple sugars.

Healthy fats were not vilified in the Mentzer Method; they were recognized as essential for hormone production and overall health. Sources of healthy fats like avocados, nuts, and olive oil were encouraged as part of a balanced diet.

Understanding macronutrients and micronutrients was a fundamental aspect of the Mentzer Method. Mike

Mentzer stressed the importance of knowing what you were putting into your body and how it would support your training goals. This knowledge allowed individuals to tailor their diets to their specific needs and goals.

In addition to whole foods, many individuals following the Mentzer Method also used supplements. Protein supplements, such as whey protein, were common additions to ensure sufficient protein intake. Creatine, a supplement known for enhancing strength and performance, was also popular among Mentzer's followers.

Hydration was not overlooked in the Mentzer Method. Staying adequately hydrated was considered essential for optimal performance and recovery. Dehydration could lead to decreased strength, fatigue, and impaired muscle function.

Mike Mentzer's approach to workout routines was not for the casual gym-goer. It demanded intensity, commitment, and a willingness to push one's limits. It favored compound exercises, short but focused workouts, and a data-driven approach to progress tracking. It emphasized the importance of rest and recovery, recognizing that muscles needed time to grow and repair. Nutrition was not an afterthought but a critical component of the training regimen, ensuring that the body had the fuel it needed to excel in the gym. In the next chapter, we will explore advanced techniques that allowed experienced lifters to take their training to the next level, pushing the boundaries of their physical capabilities. These techniques were not for the faint of heart but held the promise of exceptional results for those who dared to embrace them.

Advanced Techniques

Mike Mentzer's training philosophy was all about pushing the boundaries of what was possible in the pursuit of muscle and strength. In this chapter, we'll dive into the advanced techniques that allowed experienced lifters to take their training to the next level, challenging their bodies and minds like never before.

Intensification Techniques: Beyond Failure

While training to failure was a fundamental principle of the Mentzer Method, advanced lifters sought to push their limits even further. To achieve this, they employed intensification techniques that tested their resolve and physical capabilities.

- Forced Repetitions: This technique involved having a training partner or spotter assist in completing additional repetitions after the lifter reached muscle failure. These forced reps extended the set beyond what the individual could achieve alone, creating a deeper level of fatigue and muscle stimulation.

- Negatives: Negatives focused on the eccentric phase of an exercise, which is the lowering or lengthening portion of the movement. During negatives, lifters deliberately slowed down the descent of the weight, resisting its pull. This eccentric overload placed tremendous stress on the muscle fibers and contributed to greater muscle damage and subsequent growth.

- Partial Repetitions: Partial repetitions involved lifting a weight through a limited range of motion, often in the most challenging part of the exercise. For example, in the bench press, lifters might perform partial reps in the bottom position to target the chest muscles intensely.

These intensification techniques were not for the faint of heart. They required a high level of mental determination and often a trusted training partner to assist in their execution. But for those who were willing to embrace the challenge, these techniques could yield exceptional results, breaking through plateaus and pushing the boundaries of muscle growth.

Supersets and Drop Sets: Shocking the System

Supersets and drop sets were advanced training techniques that introduced a shock factor into the workout routine. They were particularly effective for enhancing muscle definition and improving muscular endurance.

- Supersets: Supersets involved performing two different exercises back-to-back without resting in between. These exercises could target the same muscle group or opposing muscle groups. For instance, performing a set of bench presses immediately followed by a set of bent-over rows constituted a superset.

- Drop Sets: Drop sets, also known as strip sets, involved performing a set of an exercise to failure and then immediately reducing the weight and continuing the set. This was repeated multiple times, effectively extending the duration of the set and increasing metabolic stress on the muscles.

These techniques challenged both the muscular and cardiovascular systems, fostering a unique pump and burn sensation. They were often incorporated into training routines periodically to introduce variation and shock the muscles into new growth.

Periodization: Cycling Intensity and Volume

Periodization was a strategic approach used by advanced lifters to manage training intensity and volume over time. It allowed individuals to cycle through phases of higher and lower intensity to prevent overtraining and continually challenge the body.

- Hypertrophy Phase: During this phase, lifters focused on higher volume and moderate intensity. The goal was to induce muscle hypertrophy by targeting the muscle fibers with a significant number of repetitions and sets. Exercises were selected to isolate specific muscle groups.

- Strength Phase: In the strength phase, lifters shifted their focus to heavier weights and lower repetitions. Compound movements took precedence, and the emphasis was on lifting as heavy as possible with proper form. The goal was to build raw strength and neural adaptations.

- Peaking Phase: The peaking phase occurred closer to a competition or specific goal. It involved tapering down the training volume while maintaining high intensity. The focus was on honing technique and optimizing performance for a peak effort.

Periodization allowed advanced lifters to progress systematically while minimizing the risk of overtraining or burnout. It provided a structured framework for long-term success and was a hallmark of disciplined training.

Mind-Muscle Connection: Maximizing Contraction

Advanced lifters understood the importance of the mind-muscle connection, a concept that involved consciously engaging and contracting the targeted muscle during each repetition. This connection ensured that the muscle was doing the work rather than relying solely on momentum.

To enhance the mind-muscle connection, advanced lifters often employed techniques such as:

- Slow Repetitions: Performing repetitions at a deliberately slower pace allowed lifters to focus on the muscle contraction and maximize time under tension. This increased the effectiveness of each repetition and stimulated greater muscle growth.

- Isolation Exercises: Isolation exercises were used to target specific muscles with precision. For example, performing concentration curls for the biceps allowed lifters to concentrate solely on the biceps' contraction without involvement from other muscle groups.

- Visualization: Visualization techniques involved mentally picturing the muscle working during an exercise. This mental imagery reinforced the mind-muscle connection and enhanced muscle engagement.

Advanced lifters recognized that the mind was a powerful tool in achieving optimal muscle recruitment and development. By honing the mind-muscle connection, they were able to achieve more profound contractions, leading to greater gains in strength and size.

Advanced Training Splits: Specialization and Weak Point Training

Advanced lifters often followed specialized training splits to address specific weaknesses or lagging muscle groups. These splits allowed them to allocate more time and focus to areas that needed improvement.

- Two-A-Day Workouts: Some advanced lifters incorporated two-a-day workouts, training the same muscle group in the morning and evening sessions. This intensive approach was particularly effective for lagging body parts that required additional attention.

- Specialization Phases: Specialization phases involved dedicating an entire training block to a specific muscle group or lift. For example, an advanced lifter might focus solely on squat variations for several weeks to overcome a strength plateau.

- Pre-Exhaustion: Pre-exhaustion techniques involved targeting a specific muscle group with an isolation exercise before moving on to compound movements. This approach fatigued the target muscle group, ensuring it reached failure sooner during compound exercises.

Advanced training splits and specialization allowed lifters to fine-tune their physique and address weaknesses that could hinder overall progress. They required a deep understanding of one's strengths and weaknesses and a commitment to putting in the extra work.

Functional Training: Beyond Aesthetics

While the Mentzer Method was primarily associated with bodybuilding and strength training, advanced lifters recognized the importance of functional training. Functional training focused on improving real-world movements and overall athleticism.

This approach included exercises and drills that enhanced balance, coordination, agility, and mobility. It went beyond aesthetics and catered to individuals who wanted to excel not just in the gym but in their daily lives and sports.

Injury Prevention and Recovery: Listening to the Body

Advanced lifters understood that training longevity was crucial for sustained progress. To achieve this, they paid close attention to injury prevention and recovery strategies.

- Proper Warm-Up: A thorough warm-up routine was essential to prepare the body for intense training. It included dynamic stretching, mobility drills, and activation exercises to ensure that muscles and joints were ready for action.

- Foam Rolling and Self-Myofascial Release: Foam rolling and self-myofascial release techniques were used to alleviate muscle tightness and promote blood flow. These practices reduced the risk of injury and improved recovery.

- Active Recovery: Active recovery sessions included low-intensity activities like walking, swimming, or yoga. These sessions helped flush metabolic waste from muscles, reduce soreness, and promote overall recovery.

- Listening to the Body: Perhaps the most critical aspect of injury prevention and recovery was listening to the body. Advanced lifters understood the difference between pushing through discomfort and risking injury. They knew when to adjust their training, take extra rest, or seek professional guidance when needed.

Advanced training techniques in the Mentzer Method were not for everyone. They demanded a high level of experience, dedication, and mental fortitude. These techniques allowed advanced lifters to reach new heights in muscle development, strength, and overall physical performance. But they were not pursued recklessly; they were integrated thoughtfully into training routines, taking into account individual goals and limitations.

Avoiding and Overcoming Injuries

In the world of intense, heavy lifting championed by Mike Mentzer, injuries were a lurking threat. It wasn't a matter of if, but when, injuries would rear their ugly heads. Yet, in the iron game, the ability to avoid injuries and recover from them was a testament to one's resilience and dedication. In this chapter, we'll explore the strategies and mindset required to sidestep the pitfalls of injury and come back stronger than ever.

Understanding the Risks

Before we dive into prevention and recovery strategies, it's essential to acknowledge the inherent risks in heavy training. The Mentzer Method pushed the boundaries of physical capability, demanding maximal effort and intensity in every workout. With such intensity, the risk of injuries, both acute and overuse, was always present.

- Acute Injuries: Acute injuries, such as muscle strains, ligament tears, or joint dislocations, often occurred due to sudden, forceful movements or improper technique. These injuries could happen in an instant and put individuals on the sidelines for weeks or even months.

- Overuse Injuries: Overuse injuries, on the other hand, were the result of cumulative wear and tear on the body. These injuries typically developed over time, as repetitive stress on muscles, tendons, or joints took its toll. Overuse injuries were insidious, creeping up on individuals until they became a significant hindrance to training.

- Listen to Your Body: The first line of defense against injuries was to listen to your body. It might sound simple, but many lifters ignored early warning signs of impending injury. Pain, discomfort, and reduced range of motion were signals that something was amiss. Ignoring these signals could lead to more severe injuries down the road.

- Proper Warm-Up: A thorough warm-up was non-negotiable. It prepared the body for the stresses of heavy lifting, increasing blood flow to muscles and joints and enhancing flexibility. A typical warm-up included dynamic stretching, mobility drills, and light, high-repetition sets of the exercises to be performed.

Form and Technique: The Foundations of Injury Prevention

Mike Mentzer was a stickler for proper form and technique, and for good reason. Correct form not only maximized the effectiveness of an exercise but also significantly reduced the risk of injury. Here's how form and technique played a crucial role in injury prevention:

- Controlled Movements: Every repetition should be executed with precise control. Jerky or uncontrolled movements were a recipe for disaster, inviting injury. Lifters were taught to lift and lower weights deliberately, emphasizing muscle engagement throughout the range of motion.

- Full Range of Motion: Each exercise should be performed through a full range of motion, unless specific variations were employed for specialized training. Shortening the range of motion compromised muscle activation and increased the risk of injury.

- Proper Alignment: Correct alignment of the body was critical. Misalignment placed excessive stress on joints and tendons, leading to injuries over time. Lifters were coached to maintain proper joint alignment during exercises.

- Avoiding Ego Lifts: Ego lifting, the practice of lifting weights beyond one's capabilities to impress or compete with others, was discouraged. It was a surefire way to invite injury, as the body was not adequately prepared for the load. Lifters were urged to leave their egos at the door and focus on controlled, safe lifting.

Recovery and Rehabilitation

Even with the best prevention efforts, injuries could still occur. When they did, advanced lifters approached recovery and rehabilitation with the same determination they brought to their training.

- Immediate Care: In the event of an acute injury, immediate care was crucial. This included rest, ice, compression, and elevation (RICE) for injuries like strains or sprains. For more severe injuries, seeking medical attention was paramount to assess the extent of the damage.

- Active Recovery: Active recovery was a strategy employed to promote healing while maintaining overall fitness. Low-intensity activities like swimming, walking, or cycling improved blood flow to injured areas and prevented muscle atrophy.

- Rehabilitation Exercises: Specific rehabilitation exercises were prescribed to target injured areas and gradually restore strength and function. These exercises were performed under the guidance of a qualified physical therapist or sports medicine professional.

- Patience and Persistence: Rehabilitation was not a quick fix. It required patience and persistence. Advanced lifters understood that rushing the process could lead to setbacks or re-injury. They were committed to the long-term goal of returning to full strength.

Injury Prevention: The Holistic Approach

Preventing injuries wasn't limited to proper form and technique; it was a holistic approach that encompassed various aspects of training and recovery.

- Balanced Training: Balancing muscle development was crucial. Overemphasizing one muscle group while neglecting others could lead to muscular imbalances and increase the risk of injury. The Mentzer Method encouraged a well-rounded approach to training.

- Rest and Recovery: Rest days were not signs of weakness but essential components of the training process. Adequate rest allowed the body to recover, repair, and grow. Overtraining was a common cause of injuries, and it was avoided at all costs.

- Nutrition: Proper nutrition played a significant role in injury prevention. A diet rich in nutrients, including vitamins, minerals, and antioxidants, supported overall health and immune function. Nutrient deficiencies could weaken the body's ability to recover from injuries.

- Hydration: Staying hydrated was critical for muscle function and overall health. Dehydration could lead to muscle cramps and impair performance, increasing the risk of injury.

- Supplements: While whole foods should be the foundation of one's diet, supplements could fill in nutritional gaps and support recovery. Supplements like omega-3 fatty acids and vitamin D had anti-inflammatory properties that could aid in injury prevention.

The Mental Game: Resilience and Adaptability

Injuries could be mentally challenging, often testing a lifter's resilience and adaptability. Mike Mentzer's philosophy emphasized the importance of mental strength in training, and this mindset extended to dealing with injuries.

- Positive Mindset: Maintaining a positive mindset was crucial during the recovery process. It was easy to become discouraged or frustrated when sidelined by an injury, but a positive outlook could speed up recovery and aid in the healing process.

- Adaptation: Adaptation was a fundamental concept in the Mentzer Method. Lifters understood that setbacks were part of the journey. Instead of dwelling on the injury, they adapted their training and focused on what they could do to continue progressing.

- Patience: Patience was a virtue in the world of injury recovery. Advanced lifters understood that healing took time and that rushing the process could lead to setbacks. They were willing to put in the work patiently and methodically.

Seeking Professional Help

While advanced lifters often had a deep understanding of their bodies, they also recognized the value of seeking professional help when needed. Sports medicine professionals, physical therapists, and orthopedic specialists could provide expert guidance and accelerate the recovery process.

Learning from Injuries

Injuries, while unwelcome, often held valuable lessons. Advanced lifters saw injuries as opportunities to learn more about their bodies and training. They used these unfortunate incidents as stepping stones to greater understanding and refinement of their fitness pursuits. Here are some crucial lessons that advanced lifters gleaned from injuries:

1. Listen to Your Body: Injuries served as a stark reminder of the importance of listening to one's body. Advanced lifters realized that ignoring signals of pain or discomfort could lead to severe consequences. They learned to distinguish between the discomfort of pushing boundaries and the warning signs of impending injury.

2. Prioritize Proper Form: Many injuries occurred due to poor form or technique. Advanced lifters understood that flawless execution of exercises was non-negotiable. They committed to perfecting their form, even if it meant lifting lighter weights initially. They recognized that prioritizing form not only prevented injuries but also promoted long-term progress.

3. Embrace Smart Progression: Injuries often resulted from overzealous progress or inadequate recovery. Advanced lifters adopted a more strategic approach to progression. They recognized that the body needed time to adapt, and they implemented well-structured periodization to prevent overuse injuries and burnout.

4. Focus on Prehabilitation: Prehabilitation, or injury prevention, became a priority. Advanced lifters incorporated exercises and routines designed to strengthen vulnerable areas, such as the shoulders, knees, and lower back. They viewed prehabilitation as an investment in their long-term training longevity.

5. Value Rest and Recovery: Injuries underscored the importance of rest and recovery. Advanced lifters no longer viewed rest days as signs of weakness but as

essential components of their training. They understood that recovery was when the body repaired and grew stronger, reducing the risk of injuries.

6. Seek Professional Guidance: When faced with injuries, advanced lifters didn't hesitate to seek professional guidance. They consulted physical therapists, sports medicine specialists, and experienced trainers who could provide expert advice on rehabilitation and injury prevention.

7. Mental Resilience: Injuries tested mental resilience. Advanced lifters learned to approach setbacks with a positive mindset, focusing on what they could control rather than dwelling on the limitations imposed by injuries. They channeled their mental strength into their rehabilitation and comeback.

8. Long-Term Perspective: Injuries forced advanced lifters to adopt a long-term perspective on their fitness journey. They understood that setbacks were part of the process and that patience was a virtue. They remained committed to their goals, recognizing that progress might sometimes be slower but always steady.

9. Adapt and Evolve: Finally, advanced lifters embraced adaptability. They adjusted their training routines, modified exercises, and explored new training modalities when necessary. They understood that flexibility in their approach was crucial to overcoming injuries and continuing their pursuit of excellence.

In the world of advanced lifting, injuries were not seen as defeats but as opportunities for growth and refinement. These lessons, hard-earned through trials and tribulations, made them not only physically stronger but mentally tougher athletes, ready to face any challenge that came their way on their unrelenting path to excellence.

Adapting the Method for Different Goals

The Mentzer Method, with its unapologetic focus on intensity and efficiency, was a game-changer for bodybuilders and strength enthusiasts. But what if your fitness goals extended beyond the traditional realms of bodybuilding? What if you sought to lose weight, gain muscle, or enhance your athletic performance? In this chapter, we explore how to adapt the Mentzer Method to various goals, proving that its principles can be harnessed for diverse fitness pursuits.

Adapting for Weight Loss: Shedding Pounds with Intensity

For individuals looking to shed excess weight and achieve a leaner physique, the Mentzer Method offered a potent approach that prioritized fat loss while preserving muscle mass.

- High-Intensity Cardio: High-intensity interval training (HIIT) was a powerful tool for burning calories and shedding fat. Short bursts of intense cardio, such as sprints or jump rope sessions, followed by brief periods of rest, ramped up the metabolism and incinerated body fat.

- Compound Movements: Compound exercises like squats, deadlifts, and bench presses continued to form the foundation of workouts. These compound movements engaged multiple muscle groups simultaneously, torching calories and promoting fat loss.

- Caloric Deficit: Weight loss ultimately hinged on a caloric deficit—burning more calories than consumed. Combining high-intensity workouts with a controlled, balanced diet was the recipe for success. Lifters tracked their daily caloric intake, making sure it aligned with their weight loss goals.

Adapting for Muscle Gain: Sculpting a Powerful Physique

For those aspiring to pack on muscle and sculpt a powerful physique, the Mentzer Method provided a blueprint for hypertrophy and muscle growth.

- Progressive Overload: Muscle growth was stimulated by progressively increasing the weights lifted. Lifters consistently pushed themselves to lift heavier weights or perform additional repetitions, forcing their muscles to adapt and grow.

- Isolation Exercises: While compound movements remained integral, isolation exercises could be strategically incorporated to target specific muscle groups. Bicep curls, tricep extensions, and calf raises allowed for precise muscle development.

- Periodization: Periodization, cycling through phases of higher volume and intensity, was adapted to favor hypertrophy. Hypertrophy-focused phases emphasized higher repetitions and moderate weights, maximizing time under tension for muscle growth.

Adapting for Athletic Performance: Unlocking Explosive Power

For athletes seeking to enhance their performance in sports that demanded explosive power and agility, the Mentzer Method offered a pathway to elevate their game.

- Power Exercises: Explosive power could be developed through exercises like power cleans, snatches, and plyometrics. These movements mimicked the demands of sports like football, basketball, and sprinting, enhancing speed and agility.

- Functional Training: Functional training drills and agility exercises were integrated into workouts. Ladder drills, cone drills, and agility ladder work improved coordination, balance, and agility—essential attributes for many sports.

- Periodization for Peaking: Athletes often utilized periodization to peak their performance during specific seasons or competitions. The Mentzer Method's periodization principles allowed for targeted phases of training that aligned with their competitive schedules.

Adapting for Age and Gender: Fitness for Everyone

One of the remarkable aspects of the Mentzer Method was its adaptability to different age groups and genders, debunking the myth that intense training was reserved for the young and male.

- Age Considerations: Older individuals could embrace the Mentzer Method while being mindful of their unique needs. Prioritizing joint health, incorporating flexibility work, and focusing on functional movements allowed older lifters to continue training safely and effectively.

- Gender Neutrality: The Mentzer Method was gender-neutral, with both men and women achieving remarkable results. Women, in particular, benefited from the method's focus on strength and muscle development, dispelling the notion that lifting heavy would lead to bulky physiques.

Customizing the Method: Tailoring the Mentzer Approach

One of the strengths of the Mentzer Method was its adaptability. Lifters could customize the method to suit their individual preferences and circumstances.

- Frequency of Workouts: The frequency of workouts could be adjusted to align with one's schedule and recovery capacity. Some individuals thrived on a three-day-per-week routine, while others preferred a more frequent training schedule.

- Volume and Intensity: Lifters had the flexibility to modulate training volume and intensity based on their goals and experience levels. Beginners might start with lower weights and higher repetitions, gradually progressing to heavier loads.

- Exercise Selection: The choice of exercises was not set in stone. Lifters could incorporate variations and substitutions to keep their workouts fresh and challenging. This allowed for a degree of personalization and prevented training plateaus.

Incorporating Cardiovascular Training: The Cardio Connection

While the Mentzer Method primarily revolved around resistance training, cardiovascular training could be integrated for those aiming to improve cardiovascular fitness and endurance.

- HIIT Cardio: High-intensity interval training (HIIT) was a natural fit for the Mentzer Method. Short, intense bursts of cardio, such as sprint intervals or cycling, could be interspersed with weightlifting sessions to enhance cardiovascular conditioning.

- Balancing Cardio and Strength: Finding the right balance between cardiovascular and strength training was key. Lifters could adjust the frequency and duration of cardio sessions to complement their resistance training without compromising recovery.

Nutrition and Supplementation: The Fuel for Success

No matter the fitness goal, nutrition remained a cornerstone of progress. The same principles that underpinned the Mentzer Method's training approach applied to diet and supplementation.

- Caloric Intake: Caloric intake was tailored to align with individual goals. Those seeking weight loss maintained a caloric deficit, while muscle gain required a caloric surplus. Tracking macros—

protein, carbohydrates, and fats—ensured the right nutritional balance.

- Whole Foods: Whole, unprocessed foods formed the foundation of nutrition. Lean proteins, complex carbohydrates, and healthy fats supplied the body with the necessary nutrients for energy, muscle growth, and overall health.

- Supplements for Support: While whole foods should be the primary source of nutrients, supplements could fill gaps and aid in recovery. Whey protein, creatine, and branched-chain amino acids (BCAAs) were among the supplements that supported training goals.

Consistency and Longevity: The Mentzer Way

No matter the adaptation or goal, the Mentzer Method's underlying principles of consistency, intensity, and dedication remained constant. Achieving fitness success, be it in bodybuilding, weight loss, athletic performance, or overall health, required unwavering commitment and a willingness to embrace the journey.

- The Uncompromising Path: The Mentzer Method was unapologetically intense, demanding commitment and consistency. It was not a shortcut or a quick fix but a proven path to long-term success.

- Progress Over Perfection: Lifters learned that progress, no matter how incremental, was the true measure of success. It was about becoming better than yesterday, one workout at a time.

- Adapt and Evolve: Adapting the Mentzer Method to individual goals was not a sign of weakness but a testament to its flexibility. The method evolved with the lifter, accommodating changing circumstances and aspirations.

Rational Thinking and Personal Responsibility

M ike Mentzer's philosophy hinged profoundly on the pillars of rational thinking and personal responsibility. His approach to life, deeply influenced by Ayn Rand's Objectivism, was marked by a steadfast belief in the power of the human mind and the principle of individual accountability. This chapter delves into these core aspects of Mentzer's philosophy, elucidating how they shaped not only his approach to bodybuilding but also his worldview.

Rational thinking, as espoused by Mentzer, was not merely a tool for intellectual discourse but a practical methodology for life. He believed that reason and logic were the supreme arbiters in decision-making, a conviction that stemmed from his engagement with Objectivist literature. In a 1997 interview, Mentzer stated, "Reason is man's basic means of survival. To succumb to the irrational is to deny one's nature and surrender to chaos" (Mentzer, Interview, 1997). This unwavering belief in rationality underpinned his approach to bodybuilding, where he methodically questioned and eventually overturned many of the traditional practices of the time.

Mentzer's commitment to rational thinking was evident in his meticulous approach to training and nutrition. He advocated for a scientifically grounded approach to bodybuilding, eschewing the more common empiric methods prevalent in the sport. His training regimens were based on the principle of high intensity, a concept he adopted after thorough research and experimentation. This approach was not just about lifting heavy weights; it was about understanding the physiological mechanisms that stimulate muscle growth and then applying that knowledge in the most efficient way possible.

The principle of personal responsibility was another cornerstone of Mentzer's philosophy. He firmly believed that each individual had the power and the obligation to shape their destiny. This belief was in stark contrast to the victim mentality often prevalent in society. In one of his writings, Mentzer asserted, "We are the architects of our own fate. Blaming others or external circumstances for our misfortunes is a denial of our own power and responsibility" (Mentzer, Article, 1999). This ethos of self-reliance and accountability was a recurring theme in his teachings and his life.

Mentzer often spoke about the interplay between rational thinking and personal responsibility. He posited that rational thinking enables individuals to make informed decisions, while personal responsibility ensures that they are accountable for the outcomes of those decisions. This synergy, he believed, was essential for achieving success in any endeavor. He once remarked, "Success in bodybuilding, as in life, is the result of thinking correctly and then taking responsibility for the execution of those thoughts" (Mentzer, Seminar, 1998).

In his advocacy for rational thinking, Mentzer also emphasized the importance of intellectual independence. He encouraged individuals to question popular beliefs and to seek their own truths. This stance often put him at odds with the mainstream bodybuilding community, which was rooted in long-standing traditions and practices. Mentzer's call for intellectual independence was not just a challenge to conventional wisdom; it was an invitation to personal empowerment. He believed that when individuals think for themselves, they unlock their true potential.

Mentzer's commitment to personal responsibility also extended to his views on health and wellness. He was a vocal critic of the quick-fix mentality that pervaded the fitness industry. Instead, he advocated for a long-term, sustainable approach to health, one that required individuals to take charge of their lifestyle choices. In a 2000 article, he wrote, "True health and fitness are not about finding a magic pill or a miracle diet. They are about making a series of responsible choices over time" (Mentzer, Article, 2000).

Mentzer's philosophical principles also had a profound impact on his coaching style. He was known for his direct, no-nonsense approach, often challenging his clients to think critically about their training and lifestyle habits. He didn't just provide workout routines; he sought to instill a mindset of self-discipline and intellectual rigor in his clients. His coaching was as much about building character as it was about building muscle.

Throughout his career, Mentzer remained a staunch advocate for rational thinking and personal responsibility. His writings and teachings continually emphasized these principles, making a compelling case for their relevance not just in bodybuilding but in all aspects of life. He inspired a generation of bodybuilders and fitness enthusiasts to think more deeply about their practices and to take greater control of their lives.

Mentzer's legacy, therefore, transcends the realm of physical fitness. He left behind a philosophy that champions the power of the human mind and the importance of personal agency. In a world often characterized by irrationality and abdication of responsibility, Mentzer's message stands out as a beacon of reason and empowerment. His life and work are a testament to the potential of rational thinking and personal responsibility to effect meaningful change, both in oneself and in the world.

The Philosophy of Objectivism

Mike Mentzer's alignment with Ayn Rand's philosophy of Objectivism significantly influenced his approach to bodybuilding and broader life strategy. Objectivism, a philosophical system developed by Ayn Rand, emphasizes reason, individualism, and the pursuit of one's own happiness as the highest moral purpose. For Mentzer, Rand's principles were not just abstract ideas; they were actionable guidelines that shaped his personal and professional life.

Ayn Rand, in her works, posited that reality exists independently of consciousness and that knowledge is attained through reason, a faculty that identifies and integrates the evidence of the senses. Mentzer, deeply influenced by this idea, applied rational analysis to every aspect of his training. He rejected conventional bodybuilding wisdom when it did not align with his understanding and empirical evidence. This rational approach led him to develop his high-intensity training method, a system grounded in the principles of efficiency and effectiveness. Mentzer often quoted Rand's assertion, "Reason is the only means of grasping reality and man's basic means of survival" (Rand, "Atlas Shrugged," 1957), to underline his training philosophy's basis in rational thought.

Individualism, another core tenet of Objectivism, played a significant role in Mentzer's life. Rand's philosophy promotes the idea that each individual's life belongs to them and that the pursuit of one's own happiness is the highest moral purpose. Mentzer's embodiment of this principle was evident in his unwavering commitment to his personal beliefs and methods, despite criticism from the bodybuilding community. He often said, "The individual should exist for his own sake, neither sacrificing himself to others nor sacrificing others to himself" (Mentzer, Interview, 1985). This conviction led him to advocate for personal responsibility and self-reliance, both in his training regimen and in life.

Mentzer's embrace of Objectivism extended to his view on the role of government and societal structures. Rand advocates for laissez-faire capitalism, where the rights of individuals are respected, and their interactions are voluntary. Mentzer mirrored this belief in his personal dealings and business practices, emphasizing voluntary exchange and mutual benefit. He believed that just as in the market, in bodybuilding, one should compete and trade value for value, not seek unearned advantage.

The principle of rational self-interest, a hallmark of Objectivism, was also evident in Mentzer's approach to bodybuilding and business. Rand postulated that one's own life and happiness are the ultimate values and that each individual should act in their rational self-interest. Mentzer applied this by pursuing bodybuilding not just as a sport but as a means of achieving personal fulfillment and joy. He often remarked, "To love oneself is the beginning of a lifelong romance" (Mentzer, Seminar, 1990), reflecting Rand's idea that one's own happiness and well-being should be the primary concern.

The concept of ethical egoism, as espoused by Rand, advocates that one should act in ways that genuinely benefit oneself, guided by rational principles. Mentzer's strict adherence to his training principles, despite opposition, demonstrated his commitment to ethical egoism. He believed in the pursuit of excellence for its own sake, not for external validation. His approach was encapsulated in Rand's quote, "The man who does not value himself, cannot value anything or anyone" (Rand, "The Virtue of Selfishness," 1964).

Mentzer's application of Objectivism went beyond his professional life; it was a comprehensive life strategy. He believed that the principles of reason, individualism, rational self-interest, and ethical egoism were applicable in all life aspects. This holistic approach was evident in his writings and teachings, where he encouraged others to apply these principles for personal and professional growth.

In mentoring bodybuilders and fitness enthusiasts, Mentzer emphasized the importance of thinking independently and pursuing personal goals. He encouraged his clients to critically evaluate mainstream fitness advice and to tailor their training based on rational analysis. Mentzer often remarked, "The worst curse that can befall a man is to blindly follow another's path" (Mentzer, Article, 1998). This sentiment echoes Rand's emphasis on the sovereignty of the individual's mind and the importance of personal judgment.

The influence of Objectivism in Mentzer's life extended to his views on art and aesthetics. Rand considered art as a recreation of reality according to an artist's metaphysical value judgments. Mentzer saw bodybuilding as an art form, where the body was the canvas, and the weights were the brush. He believed in creating a physique that represented his values and ideals, not conforming to external standards of beauty or appeal. This artistic expression was grounded in the Objectivist belief in the integration of man's spirit and body.

Mike Mentzer's alignment with Ayn Rand's Objectivism profoundly influenced his approach to bodybuilding and his broader life philosophy. The principles of reason, individualism, rational self-interest, and ethical egoism not only shaped his training methods but also his worldview. Mentzer's life serves as a testament to the practical application of Objectivism, demonstrating its relevance and efficacy in both personal and professional realms.

Discipline and Determination

Mike Mentzer's philosophy, deeply rooted in discipline and determination, was a fundamental element in his approach to fitness and life. His belief in the power of disciplined action and unwavering determination shaped not only his bodybuilding career but also his broader worldview.

Discipline, for Mentzer, was not just a practice; it was a way of life. He believed that success in any field, be it bodybuilding, business, or personal endeavors, required a disciplined approach. This meant consistent, dedicated effort towards a goal, regardless of the obstacles. Mentzer's own training regimen was a testament to this principle. He trained with intense focus and precision, adhering strictly to his high-intensity training methodology. This discipline extended beyond the gym; he was meticulous about his diet, rest, and recovery, understanding that these were crucial components of his overall training program.

Mentzer often emphasized that discipline should be self-imposed, a product of one's own rational decision-making process. He believed that discipline imposed from the outside was less effective and often counterproductive. He once said, "True discipline comes from within. It's the result of consciously deciding what is worth pursuing and then committing yourself fully to the pursuit" (Mentzer, Interview, 1996). This perspective reflects a deep understanding of human psychology and the importance of personal commitment in achieving success.

Determination was another key aspect of Mentzer's philosophy. He believed that determination was the driving force that propelled an individual towards their goals, especially in the face of adversity. Mentzer's own journey in the world of bodybuilding was marked by numerous challenges, yet his determination never wavered. He was often at odds with the prevailing bodybuilding norms and faced skepticism and criticism for his unconventional methods. Despite this, he remained steadfast in his beliefs and continued to advocate for his high-intensity training approach.

Mentzer's determination was deeply intertwined with his commitment to rational thinking. He believed that a determined mindset stemmed from a clear understanding of one's goals and the logical steps required to achieve them. This rational approach to determination was evident in his training philosophy, where every exercise and routine was chosen for its effectiveness and efficiency. Mentzer once remarked, "Determination is not just about stubborn persistence. It's about understanding your goals and the most rational way to achieve them" (Mentzer, Seminar, 1997).

The interplay between discipline and determination in Mentzer's philosophy was evident in his approach to overcoming obstacles. He viewed challenges not as insurmountable barriers but as opportunities to apply disciplined thought and determined action. This mindset was crucial in his ability to continually refine and adapt his training methods, always striving for greater efficiency and effectiveness.

Mentzer's emphasis on discipline and determination had a profound impact on his coaching and mentoring style. He encouraged his clients to develop these qualities, not just for their fitness goals but for all aspects of their lives. He often said, "The discipline and determination you build in the gym can and should be applied to all areas of your life" (Mentzer, Article, 1998). This statement reflects his belief in the universal applicability of these principles.

Mentzer's application of discipline and determination extended beyond personal development; it was also a key component of his business practices. In his dealings, he was known for his integrity, reliability, and commitment to his principles. This disciplined approach to business earned him respect and admiration in the fitness industry and beyond.

The principles of discipline and determination were not just theoretical concepts for Mentzer; they were practical tools that he used to navigate the complexities of life. He understood that achieving any significant goal required a disciplined approach and the determination to see it through, regardless of the difficulties encountered along the way.

In summary, discipline and determination were foundational elements of Mike Mentzer's philosophy. These qualities were evident in every aspect of his life, from his rigorous training routines to his business dealings and personal endeavors. Mentzer's disciplined approach to bodybuilding, combined with his unwavering determination, made him a legendary figure in the fitness world and a role model for those seeking to achieve excellence in their own lives. His legacy is a testament to the power of disciplined thought and determined action in the pursuit of one's goals.

Achieving Excellence and Success

I n the philosophy of Mike Mentzer, the concepts of excellence and success were not mere abstract ideals but tangible objectives attainable through a combination of mental fortitude, rational thought, and disciplined effort. Mentzer's views on achieving excellence and success were deeply influenced by his experiences in bodybuilding, but they extended far beyond the confines of the sport.

For Mentzer, success was not merely winning competitions or achieving a certain physique; it was about the pursuit and attainment of personal goals, whatever they might be. He believed that success was an individual concept, defined differently by each person. "Success is about achieving what you personally find meaningful, not what others deem significant," he often remarked (Mentzer, Interview, 1995). This perspective underscored the importance he placed on individual values and goals in the pursuit of success.

Excellence, in Mentzer's view, was closely related to success but with a distinct nuance. It was about constantly striving to improve, to surpass one's previous achievements. Excellence was a dynamic process, not a static state. Mentzer applied this concept to his training, constantly seeking to refine his methods and improve his physique. But more importantly, he applied it to his life, always aiming to better himself in various aspects. "Excellence is a journey, not a destination. It's about continuously pushing your limits," he stated in a seminar (Mentzer, Seminar, 1996).

Mentzer's approach to achieving excellence and success was grounded in a strong mindset. He believed that mental fortitude was the key to overcoming challenges and obstacles. This belief was born out of his experiences in bodybuilding, where mental strength was as important as physical strength. He often faced skepticism and criticism for his unconventional training methods, but his mental resilience allowed him to persevere and ultimately succeed.

One of the key components of Mentzer's mindset was the ability to deal with failure. He did not view failure as a setback but as a learning opportunity. "Every failure is a step towards success if you learn from it," he would say (Mentzer, Article, 1998). This attitude towards failure was crucial in his pursuit of excellence, as it allowed him to take risks and try new approaches without the fear of failing.

Another important aspect of Mentzer's mindset was his focus on rational thinking. He believed that success and excellence were achieved through logical and analytical thought processes. This rational approach was evident in the way he designed his training programs, carefully analyzing each exercise's effectiveness and efficiency. But it also applied to his life decisions, where he would weigh the pros and cons and make choices based on reason rather than emotion.

Mentzer also emphasized the importance of discipline in achieving success and excellence. He believed that without discipline, talent and potential were wasted. Discipline, to Mentzer, meant more than just showing up; it meant giving your best effort in every endeavor. "Discipline is the bridge between goals and accomplishment," he would often say in interviews (Mentzer, Interview, 1999).

In addition to mental fortitude, rational thinking, and discipline, Mentzer also believed in the power of persistence. He understood that the path to success and excellence was often long and fraught with challenges. Persistence was what kept you on the path, even when the going got tough. "Persistence is the key to breaking barriers. It's what separates the achievers from the quitters," he said in a motivational speech (Mentzer, Speech, 1997).

Mentzer's philosophy on achieving excellence and success was not just theoretical; it was a reflection of his life. He applied these principles in his bodybuilding career, his business ventures, and his personal life. His achievements in bodybuilding, despite the odds stacked against him, were a testament to the efficacy of his philosophy.

Mike Mentzer's views on achieving excellence and success were an integral part of his philosophy. They were principles that he lived by and advocated for in his teachings and writings. His approach to success and excellence – characterized by mental fortitude, rational thinking, discipline, and persistence – is a powerful guide for anyone seeking to achieve their personal and professional goals.

Health, Wellness, and Longevity

Mike Mentzer's approach to health, wellness, and longevity transcended the typical boundaries of bodybuilding and fitness. His philosophy was comprehensive, emphasizing the interconnectedness of physical health, mental well-being, and overall life satisfaction. Mentzer believed that a holistic approach was essential for achieving not only a great physique but also a fulfilling life.

Physical health was, unsurprisingly, a cornerstone of Mentzer's philosophy. However, his views on maintaining physical health went beyond the conventional focus on exercise and muscle building. He understood that physical health was a complex interplay of various factors, including diet, rest, and the type of exercise. "Physical health isn't just about lifting weights. It's about nurturing the body with the right nutrients, allowing adequate rest, and engaging in exercises that promote overall well-being," Mentzer noted in a 1995 interview (Mentzer, 1995).

Diet was a particularly important aspect of Mentzer's approach to health. He advocated for a balanced diet that provided the necessary nutrients for muscle growth and overall health. This included a focus on high-quality proteins, complex carbohydrates, and healthy fats. Mentzer was critical of fad diets or extreme nutritional regimens that were popular in bodybuilding circles. He believed that such approaches were not sustainable and could be detrimental in the long run. "A diet should be as rational as your training. It's about giving your body what it needs, not depriving or overloading it," he advised in a seminar (Mentzer, Seminar, 1997).

Rest and recovery were also integral to Mentzer's health philosophy. He was a strong advocate for giving the body time to recover from the stresses of training. This was not only to prevent injury but also to ensure that the muscles had time to grow. Mentzer often pointed out the counterproductivity of overtraining, which was a common practice among bodybuilders. "Rest is not a luxury; it's a vital part of your training regimen," he often reminded his followers (Mentzer, Article, 1998).

Mentzer's holistic approach extended to mental well-being, which he believed was closely linked to physical health. He understood that mental stress could have detrimental effects on the body and that a healthy mind was essential for a healthy body. Mentzer often incorporated meditation and relaxation techniques into his routine, advocating these practices to his followers. "The mind and body are interconnected. Neglecting the health of one affects the other," he stated in an article (Mentzer, Article, 2000).

Longevity was another key aspect of Mentzer's health philosophy. He believed that the goal of fitness should not be limited to short-term gains but should include long-term health and vitality. This long-term view influenced his training methods, which emphasized sustainability and safety. Mentzer discouraged practices that promised quick results at the expense of long-term health. "The goal is to build a body that is strong, healthy, and functional for years to come, not just for the next competition," he emphasized in a public lecture (Mentzer, Lecture, 1999).

In his recommendations for a healthy lifestyle, Mentzer often focused on practical and sustainable practices. This included regular physical activity that one enjoyed, a balanced diet, adequate sleep, and stress management. He was critical of extreme measures and quick fixes, whether in diet, exercise, or lifestyle changes. "Health is not about extreme measures. It's about making smart, sustainable choices every day," he advised in a magazine interview (Mentzer, Magazine Interview, 1998).

Mentzer's approach to health, wellness, and longevity was reflective of his overall philosophy of life. It was rational, balanced, and holistic. He understood that the pursuit of health was not just about looking good but about feeling good and living well. His teachings in this area continue to influence the fitness world, offering a more balanced and sustainable approach to health and well-being.

In conclusion, Mike Mentzer's holistic approach to health, wellness, and longevity was a vital component of his overall philosophy. He emphasized the interconnectedness of physical and mental health and advocated for sustainable practices that promoted long-term well-being. His approach was a departure from the more extreme and short-sighted practices prevalent in the bodybuilding community, offering a more rational and balanced path to achieving health and longevity.

Critiques and Controversies

Mike Mentzer's approach to bodybuilding and his broader philosophical stance, while revolutionary, were not without their critics. His ideas, especially his advocacy of high-intensity training and his alignment with Objectivism, sparked controversy and debate within the bodybuilding community and beyond. This chapter examines these critiques, along with Mentzer's responses, to provide a comprehensive understanding of his methods and philosophy.

A primary critique of Mentzer's methodology was his staunch advocacy of high-intensity training (HIT). Critics argued that his approach was too extreme and that it could lead to overtraining and injury. They contended that the body requires more frequent and varied stimulus for optimal muscle growth, which Mentzer's approach did not provide. "Mentzer's high-intensity training is overly rigid and ignores the body's need for varied stimulus," one critic noted in a 1998 issue of a bodybuilding magazine (Bodybuilding Magazine, 1998). Critics also pointed out that HIT was not suitable for everyone, especially beginners who might not have the capacity to handle such intense workouts.

Mentzer, in response to these criticisms, emphasized the scientific basis of his training methodology. He argued that HIT was not only effective but also efficient, offering maximum results in minimum time. He pointed to the success of many who followed his program, including himself, as evidence of its efficacy. "My training methodology is grounded in science. It's about working smarter, not harder," Mentzer stated in a 1999 interview (Mentzer, Interview, 1999). He also noted that his approach was adaptable and that he often customized the training intensity and frequency based on the individual's capacity and goals.

Another area of critique was Mentzer's alignment with Ayn Rand's philosophy of Objectivism. Critics argued that Objectivism's focus on individualism and rational self-interest was too extreme and could lead to selfishness and a lack of empathy. They contended that such a philosophy was antithetical to the principles of community and cooperation, which are also important in the bodybuilding world. "Mentzer's embrace of Objectivism promotes a self-centered worldview that can be detrimental in a community-based sport like bodybuilding," a critic argued in a 2001 fitness journal article (Fitness Journal, 2001).

Mentzer's defense of Objectivism was robust. He believed that Objectivism's emphasis on rational self-interest and individualism did not equate to selfishness or a lack of empathy. Instead, he argued that it promoted personal responsibility and self-improvement, which ultimately benefited both the individual and the community. "Objectivism advocates for rational self-interest, which is not about being selfish. It's about recognizing and fulfilling your potential, which in turn allows you to contribute more effectively to society," he explained in a book on bodybuilding philosophy (Mentzer, Book on Bodybuilding Philosophy, 2000).

Mentzer also faced criticism for his sometimes dogmatic approach to training and philosophy. Some critics felt that he was too rigid in his beliefs and unwilling to consider alternative viewpoints. They argued that this dogmatism was counterproductive, especially in a field like bodybuilding, where new research and methods are constantly emerging. "Mentzer's rigid adherence to his methods and philosophy stifles innovation and adaptation, which are crucial in the ever-evolving field of bodybuilding," a fellow bodybuilder commented in a 2002 interview (Fellow Bodybuilder, Interview, 2002).

In response to these criticisms, Mentzer acknowledged that while he was confident in his methods and philosophy, he was open to new ideas and research. He clarified that his approach was based on current scientific understanding and his own experiences, both of which were subject to change with new evidence. "I am committed to my methods and philosophy because they are based on what I know to be true. However, I am always willing to consider new evidence and adapt accordingly," he stated in a 2003 seminar (Mentzer, Seminar, 2003).

In summary, while Mike Mentzer's methods and philosophical stance were groundbreaking and influential, they were not without their critiques. These critiques ranged from the practical implications of his training methodology to the philosophical underpinnings of his approach. Mentzer's responses to these critiques highlighted his commitment to his principles while also acknowledging the importance of adaptability and openness to new ideas. The debate surrounding his methods and philosophy underscores the dynamic nature of the bodybuilding field and the complexity of finding a one-size-fits-all approach.

Mentzer's Legacy and Influence

The legacy and influence of Mike Mentzer extend far beyond the confines of the bodybuilding stage. His innovative approach to fitness, combined with his philosophical insights, has left a profound impact on contemporary thinkers and continues to influence future generations. This chapter delves into the multifaceted nature of Mentzer's legacy, examining the breadth and depth of his influence in various domains.

Mike Mentzer revolutionized the world of bodybuilding with his high-intensity training (HIT) methodology. His approach, which emphasized efficiency, intensity, and scientific underpinning, challenged the prevailing bodybuilding paradigms of his time. Mentzer's HIT became a foundational principle for many subsequent training programs and has been credited with influencing a generation of bodybuilders and fitness enthusiasts. His famous quote, "It is the quality of effort, not the quantity, which is responsible for growth stimulation," (Mentzer, Bodybuilding Seminar, 1993) encapsulates the essence of his training philosophy.

Mentzer's influence, however, was not limited to training methodologies. His philosophical approach to bodybuilding, grounded in Ayn Rand's Objectivism, introduced a new dimension to the sport. He advocated for a rational, principled approach to training and life, emphasizing the importance of individual thought and personal responsibility. His alignment with Objectivism resonated with many in the bodybuilding community, encouraging them to think more deeply about their motivations and methods. "The person who can think and act on his own is the person who will be successful in bodybuilding and in life," Mentzer asserted in a 1996 interview (Mentzer, Interview, 1996).

Mentzer's legacy is also evident in his critique of the bodybuilding industry. He was vocal about the dangers of steroid abuse and the unrealistic expectations set by the industry. His advocacy for natural bodybuilding and his critical view of performance-enhancing drugs were ahead of his time and influenced the industry's gradual shift towards health and sustainability. "Bodybuilding should be about health and vitality, not just aesthetics," Mentzer remarked during a conference in 1998 (Mentzer, Conference, 1998).

Beyond bodybuilding, Mentzer's philosophies found resonance in broader life strategies and personal development. His emphasis on rational thinking, self-discipline, and personal responsibility has influenced not just athletes but individuals in various fields. Mentzer's teachings on goal setting, overcoming obstacles, and pursuing excellence have been applied in business, personal coaching, and self-help. His approach to life challenges - analytical, disciplined, and principled - has inspired many to adopt a more thoughtful and systematic approach to their personal and professional lives.

Mentzer's writings and seminars have also had a lasting educational impact. His books, articles, and public speaking engagements were not just about imparting training techniques; they were also platforms for discussing broader philosophical ideas. Through these mediums, Mentzer challenged his audience to think critically and to question conventional wisdom. "Don't accept things at face value; analyze and make your own conclusions," he often encouraged his readers and listeners (Mentzer, Book Signing, 2001).

In the realm of health and wellness, Mentzer's holistic approach to fitness – incorporating mental and physical well-being – has been increasingly adopted in contemporary fitness philosophies. His understanding of the interplay between mental health, physical health, and overall life satisfaction has influenced current trends that emphasize a more balanced approach to fitness and health.

Furthermore, Mentzer's influence extends to the realm of coaching and mentorship. His approach to coaching was characterized by a deep commitment to his clients' success, both in and out of the gym. He was known for his ability to motivate and inspire, pushing his clients to not only achieve their fitness goals but also to realize their personal potential. His legacy lives on in the many coaches and trainers who were influenced by his methods and who continue to apply his principles in their work.

In summary, Mike Mentzer's legacy is a rich tapestry of innovative training methods, philosophical insights, and a holistic approach to health and fitness. His influence extends beyond the realm of bodybuilding, touching upon various aspects of life and personal development. Mentzer's teachings continue to inspire and guide those seeking a rational, disciplined, and principled approach to their endeavors. His impact on the bodybuilding world and his contributions to broader discussions on health, fitness, and personal development have secured his place as a pivotal figure in the history of fitness and wellness.

Mentzer's Principles in Daily Life

Implementing Mike Mentzer's principles in daily life requires a comprehensive understanding of his philosophy, which combines elements of high-intensity training, rational thinking, individual responsibility, and a holistic approach to wellness. These principles can be applied not only in fitness but also in various aspects of daily life. This practical guide aims to translate Mentzer's philosophy into actionable steps, making it accessible and applicable for those seeking to incorporate his teachings into their lifestyle.

1. Embracing High-Intensity Training Principles in Exercise:

Mentzer's high-intensity training (HIT) advocates for brief, infrequent, and intense workouts. To implement this in your exercise routine, focus on performing a few exercises per workout, each with full effort and to the point of muscle fatigue. Remember Mentzer's words, "It's not about the number of hours you spend in the gym, it's about the effort you put in" (Mentzer, Interview, 2000). Each exercise should be performed with proper form, a controlled pace, and without unnecessary movements.

2. Applying Rational Thinking to Decision Making:

Rational thinking, a key aspect of Mentzer's philosophy, involves making decisions based on logical analysis rather than emotion or societal pressures. In daily life, this could mean critically assessing the information you receive, whether it's news, advice from others, or even your own long-held beliefs. Question the validity and source of the information, analyze its relevance to your situation, and make decisions based on objective evidence. As Mentzer often said, "Think critically and make informed decisions" (Mentzer, Seminar, 2001).

3. Cultivating Personal Responsibility:

Personal responsibility, a cornerstone of Mentzer's approach, entails taking ownership of your actions and their outcomes. This involves setting personal goals, creating a plan to achieve them, and holding yourself accountable. In practice, this means not blaming external factors for your failures or shortcomings, but instead looking inward to understand how your actions contributed to the outcome. Mentzer emphasized, "You are the master of your destiny, take charge of it" (Mentzer, Article, 1999).

4. Integrating a Holistic Approach to Health:

Mentzer advocated for a holistic approach to health that includes physical, mental, and emotional well-being. To incorporate this into your life, balance your fitness routine with activities that support mental health, such as meditation, reading, or engaging in hobbies. Nutrition also plays a vital role; follow a balanced diet that provides necessary nutrients without resorting to extreme or fad diets. Mentzer believed in the interconnectedness of all aspects of health, often stating, "Health is holistic; a healthy mind resides in a healthy body" (Mentzer, Book, 2002).

5. Embracing Longevity in Fitness and Life Choices:

Mentzer's approach to longevity involves making choices that support long-term health and well-being. This includes avoiding quick fixes in fitness, such as steroids or other harmful substances, and instead focusing on sustainable practices. Similarly, in life, opt for habits and choices that promote long-term well-being, such as regular health check-ups, avoiding harmful substances like tobacco, and maintaining a balance between work and rest.

6. Implementing Structured and Disciplined Life Practices:

Discipline, a key element in Mentzer's philosophy, can be applied to everyday routines. Create structured schedules for your day, allotting specific times for work, exercise, meals, and relaxation. Adhere to these schedules diligently, understanding that discipline is crucial for achieving long-term goals. Mentzer often remarked, "Discipline in all aspects of life leads to success" (Mentzer, Interview, 1998).

7. Applying Objectivism in Personal Development:

Implementing Objectivism in personal development involves focusing on self-improvement and personal growth based on rational self-interest. This means pursuing goals that align with your values and interests, continuously seeking knowledge and skills that enhance your life, and engaging in productive and fulfilling activities.

8. Practicing Mindfulness and Stress Management:

Mentzer's holistic approach includes managing stress and practicing mindfulness. Incorporate stress-reduction techniques such as deep breathing, yoga, or mindfulness meditation into your daily routine. Remember that mental health is as important as physical health in overall well-being.

9. Seeking Continuous Improvement and Learning:

Mentzer's philosophy of continuous improvement can be applied to lifelong learning. Be open to new experiences and knowledge, seek opportunities for growth, and never become complacent. As Mentzer advised, "Always be a student, willing to learn and improve" (Mentzer, Lecture, 1997).

10. Engaging in Community and Mentorship:

Despite his emphasis on individualism, Mentzer also recognized the value of community and mentorship. Engage with others who share your interests, seek mentors who can guide you, and be willing to mentor others. As he stated, "Sharing knowledge and

Mentzer Philosophies Applied to Training

Mike Mentzer's Heavy Duty training system revolutionized bodybuilding with its high-intensity training (HIT) approach, significantly impacting the sport even decades after its introduction. This system, heavily influenced by Arthur Jones' HIT philosophy, was Mentzer's unique interpretation and expansion into a more radical regimen. Mentzer's philosophy was not just about lifting weights; it was a holistic approach encompassing training, nutrition, and mindset, tailored for both professional bodybuilders and average, drug-free individuals striving for their natural muscular potential.

The cornerstone of Mentzer's training philosophy was intensity. He defined intensity as "the percentage of possible momentary muscular effort being exerted," emphasizing the need to push muscles to their absolute limit. For Mentzer, the key to muscle hypertrophy was not the volume of exercise but the intensity. He believed in reaching as close to 100% exertion as possible during reps to stimulate muscle growth. This approach was corroborated by scientific research, which highlighted the role of mechanical tension in muscle growth. Mentzer's description of the "last rep" showcases his philosophy vividly - the final, nearly impossible repetition, full of exertion, was seen as crucial in triggering the body's muscle growth mechanisms.

To achieve this high level of intensity, Mentzer incorporated techniques like pre-exhausting muscle groups, assisted lifting, and holding weights at different points during the lift. These methods were designed to bring the bodybuilder closer to muscle failure more quickly, thus maximizing muscle growth potential. The emphasis was on reaching failure with each exercise, a principle central to the Heavy Duty method.

Another pivotal aspect of Mentzer's philosophy was low workout volume. He argued against the then-prevailing notion that more volume in weight training was better. Instead, Mentzer suggested a low volume approach, emphasizing that fewer reps with heavier weight could achieve the necessary intensity for muscle growth more effectively than numerous reps with lighter weight. This approach was not just about efficiency in training; it also allowed bodybuilders time for other pursuits, like studying or art, reflecting Mentzer's holistic view of bodybuilding as part of a balanced life. Initially, Mentzer prescribed 1 to 2 sets of 6 to 8 reps for each exercise, performed to failure. The goal was to increase the weight by 10% once 12 reps could be achieved in a set, thus maintaining the challenge and intensity.

Mentzer also stressed the importance of low frequency in workouts. He believed that recovery was crucial since muscles grow from the stimulus of weightlifting during the recovery phase. In his most extreme version of Heavy Duty, he recommended performing 1 to 2 sets for a muscle group just once a week, allowing the other six days for recovery. This perspective was rooted in the understanding that recovery is as essential as the workout itself for muscle growth. The idea was to provide enough stimulus during the workout to promote growth, but then to allow ample time for the body to recover and adapt.

Mike Mentzer's training philosophy, epitomized by his Heavy Duty system, represented a significant shift from traditional bodybuilding methods. It emphasized the quality of the workout over quantity, focusing on intensity, low volume, and sufficient recovery. This approach was tailored to maximize muscle growth in the most efficient and effective way possible, challenging the conventional wisdom of the bodybuilding world at the time. Mentzer's legacy continues through the athletes and trainers who adopt and adapt his principles, proving the enduring impact of his revolutionary ideas on the world of bodybuilding.

Made in the USA
Las Vegas, NV
23 April 2024

89036594R00085